portuguese
grammar
sue tyson-ward

For Mum, Dad and Ed.

For UK order enquiries: please contact Bookpoint Ltd, 130 Milton Park, Abingdon, Oxon OX14 4SB. Telephone: +44 (0) 1235 827720. Fax: +44 (0) 1235 400454. Lines are open 09.00–18.00, Monday to Saturday, with a 24-hour message answering service. Details about our titles and how to order are available at www.teachyourself.co.uk

For USA order enquiries: please contact McGraw-Hill Customer Services, PO Box 545, Blacklick, OH 43004-0545, USA. Telephone: 1-800-722-4726. Fax: 1-614-755-5645.

For Canada order enquiries: please contact McGraw-Hill Ryerson Ltd, 300 Water St, Whitby, Ontario L1N 9B6, Canada. Telephone: 905 430 5000. Fax: 905 430 5020.

Long renowned as the authoritative source for self-guided learning – with more than 40 million copies sold worldwide – the **teach yourself** series includes over 300 titles in the fields of languages, crafts, hobbies, business, computing and education.

British Library Cataloguing in Publication Data: a catalogue record for this title is available from the British Library.

Library of Congress Catalog Card Number: on file.

First published in UK 2003 by Hodder Education, 338 Euston Road, London, NW1 3BH.

First published in US 2003 by Contemporary Books, a Division of the McGraw-Hill Companies, 1 Prudential Plaza, 130 East Randolph Street, Chicago, IL 60601 USA.

This edition published 2003.

The **teach yourself** name is a registered trade mark of Hodder Headline.

Copyright © 2003 Sue Tyson-Ward

Typeset by Transet Limited, Coventry, England.
Printed in Great Britain for Hodder Education, a division of Hodder Headline, 338 Euston Road, London NW1 3BH, by Cox & Wyman Ltd, Reading, Berkshire.

Hodder Headline's policy is to use papers that are natural, renewable and recyclable products and made from wood grown in sustainable forests. The logging and manufacturing processes are expected to conform to the environmental regulations of the country of origin.

Impression number   10 9 8 7 6
Year   2010 2009 2008 2007 2006

iii

contents

the basics of Portuguese spelling • differences
between European and Brazilian Portuguese
• punctuation • accents • stress

gender: masculine and feminine words • number:
how to form plurals • articles • uses of the
definite article • omission of articles • neuter
article *o* • noun ellipsis

agreement of adjectives depending on gender
and number • position of adjectives • suffixes
• a selection of common descriptive adjectives

formation of adverbs • avoiding the use of *-mente*

how to compare adjectives • expressing
equality and inequality • how to compare
adverbs

pointing things and people out with demonstrative
adjectives • demonstrative pronouns

possessive adjectives • possessive pronouns

introduction

This book is intended as a reference guide for those who, with or without the help of a teacher, wish to study the essentials of Portuguese grammar.

The beginner will find that all main linguistic terms are explained in the glossary at the start of the book, and all structures are illustrated with examples that are translated into English. It is probably worthwhile making the **Glossary** your starting point, especially if you are unsure about terms such as noun, verb, adverb, etc. The more advanced student will be able to progress at a faster pace, either by working through the units in chronological order, or by dipping into units where practice is required.

The structure of the units is explained in the next section, but you should find each one clearly signposted and easy to navigate. The provision of exercises and lively activities in each unit allows students to test their understanding of the material covered, and all answers are given in the **Key** at the end of the book. A regular small amount of grammar and vocabulary learning, every day if possible, will enable students to establish firm linguistic foundations. A good dictionary will also be useful to refer to in conjunction with this book.

Acknowledgements

I would like to thank the following people involved in the production of this book:

Sue Hart and Rebecca Green at Hodder, for their continued support, guidance and hard work; Michelle Armstrong and Ginny Catmur at Hodder, for their excellent editing work; Phil

Turk and the readers, for their useful comments and advice; Francisco Fernandes, for his insightful guidance; my students, for trying out many of the exercises; my husband Ed, for his patience through yet another winter of writing, whilst maintaining a steady supply of hot drinks and chocolate; and finally, my Mum, for keeping the house clean for me whilst I sat at my desk.

how to use this book

A glossary of gramatical terms follows this section for easy reference whenever the explanation of a term is required. Each of the 46 units – with the exception of the first – consists of the following sections:

- Grammar in focus
- Exercises
- Grammar in context

The following is a suggestion as to how you might sensibly work through each unit:

Read through the **Grammar in focus** section, where the language point of the unit is explained with examples (translated into English). See if you can think of any further examples yourself. You may also find it useful to start making a list of new words (vocabulary) you come across in the examples. Most people find it easier to write vocabulary in a separate notebook – try to list words by topic areas, and add to it all the time, even when you are on holiday!

When the structures listed are clear to you, try out the exercises that follow the explanations. These are designed to give you immediate practice of the grammar points, through a variety of activities – completing sentences, re-arranging words, puzzles and other lively exercises. 'Grammar' does not have to mean 'dull'! It may well be better not to write your answers into the book, so that you can return to the exercises at a later date to test yourself. At that point, try to do them without looking at the explanations, to see what you can remember.

Proceed on to the **Grammar in context** section, where you will find the structures of the unit illustrated in realistic texts such as dialogues, extracts from brochures or newspapers, and resources such as tickets and timetables. You will find some help with vocabulary and a few questions to guide you through comprehension of the text.

At certain points in the book you will find **Language watch** boxes. These point out links between Portuguese and English (and other languages), and are full of handy hints to aid your learning of Portuguese.

Whilst the book takes European Portuguese as its standard, where there are major differences in structure or vocabulary in Brazilian Portuguese, these are highlighted. There is also an overview of different words on page 261. Anyone intending to use their Portuguese in Portuguese-speaking Africa or East Timor would be advised to request information on local vocabulary from contacts/organizations inside the relevant country. See also the **Taking it further** section.

At the end of the book you will find comprehensive verb tables, a list of useful language websites and additional advice in **Taking it further**, and the **Key** to all the exercises.

There are clear explanations of the structures of the Portuguese language although, to ease comprehension, and therefore progress, of the student, grammatical terminology has been kept to a minimum.

glossary of grammatical terms

Grammar is nothing to fear! Many people have an aversion to the word itself, as they may remember bad experiences of early (dull) learning, or perceive it as generally 'difficult' or 'irrelevant'. However, you cannot adequately learn a language without studying the grammar, in whatever guise that might be. Grammar is simply the building blocks which, once linked together, make up the framework of the language, enabling you to do something more than simply churn out travel phrases parrot-fashion. The main basic terms are explained simply below, with examples in English. You can refer back to these notes at any time whilst you are studying.

accents these are written marks above letters which affect either how that letter is pronounced, or at what point the word should be stressed (emphasized) when spoken. An accent can also be used to differentiate between two words with identical spellings but with different meanings. English does not use written accents (apart from on foreign words imported into the language), but many other languages do. See Unit 1 for more on accents in Portuguese.

adjectives words which describe or give more information about nouns. In Portuguese adjectives match their endings to the nouns they are linked with (e.g. showing whether they are singular / plural or masculine / feminine), e.g. *a lovely cup of tea, that expensive coat.*

adverbs these are words which describe, or tell us more about how an action (verb) is carried out. They often answer the question *How?* They are also used to describe adjectives more fully. Often in English, an adverb has the ending *-ly* on it, e.g. *He sings sweetly. They are incredibly clever*

agreement when related words, e.g. nouns and adjectives, have the same endings.

articles words which go with nouns. **Definite** articles are the words for *the*, and **indefinite** articles are the words for *a, an, some*. In Portuguese there are different words corresponding to the number and gender of a noun (whether it is masculine or feminine).

auxiliary verb a verb used in conjunction with another verb to form a different **tense** or the passive **voice** (see below).

cardinal numbers numbers one, two, three etc.

clause a group of words containing a verb, e.g. *before we go out ..., if she swims fast...*

colloquial a more casual, familiar style of spoken language.

comparative form of adjectives and adverbs used to make comparisons, e.g. *fatter, more slowly.*

compound tense a verb tense made up of more than one verb form, e.g. *he has gone, we will have won.*

conjugate what you do to a verb when you change its endings to denote person and tense, e.g. *we write, she writes, I wrote.*

conjunction word which is used to join together other words, phrases or clauses, e.g. *and, but, because.*

demonstratives the words used for pointing things out – *this, that, these, those.*

determiner the term for words which can precede a noun, such as articles (definite and indefinite), possessives and demonstratives.

direct speech the exact words someone has spoken, usually contained within speech marks, and introduced by expressions such as *She said..., I asked...*

idiom, idiomatic expression which is not easily directly translated into another language, and often does not relate to normal rules of grammar, e.g. *raining cats and dogs.*

imperative a form of the verb, known as a mood, used when giving commands.

impersonal verb a verb used in the 'it' form, e.g. *It is raining.* There are a number of these in Portuguese.

indicative mood the normal form of the verb used for straightforward statements, questions and negatives.

indirect speech reported speech, or speech where the exact words of the original statement are not necessarily used, and where speech marks are not required, e.g. *He said that he would not do it.*

infinitive the part of the verb referred to in English as *to...*, and the form found in the dictionary.

inflection change to the form of a word (noun, adjective etc.), to denote person, number, tense, mood or voice.

interrogatives question forms, e.g. *Where? Which?*

modal verbs verb used in conjunction with another verb in order to express a 'mood', such as wanting, liking, obligation, ability and possibility. e.g. *I **would** like to go home. **Could** you take me?*

mood verbs are divided into three usage groups, each of which uses its own particular endings across a range of tenses: indicative (expressing fact), subjunctive (non-factual or contrary to fact), and imperative (commands).

negative the expression of ideas such as *no, not, never, no one* etc.

nouns a noun is any thing, person or abstract idea in existence – everything around us is a noun of some kind. A noun can be singular (just one), or plural (more than one). In Portuguese nouns are also divided into masculine and feminine words, e.g. *table, horses, man–men, happiness*

number whether a word is singular (just one), or plural (more than one).

object The person or thing on the receiving end of the action of a verb. Objects can be 'direct', i.e. they directly receive the action of the verb, or 'indirect', where they receive the results of the action through indirect means.
e.g. *She gives **money** every week.* (*Money* is the direct object.)
*She gives **them** money every week.* (*Them* is the indirect object.)

ordinal number first, second, third etc.

past participle together with an auxiliary verb forms certain compound tenses (tenses made up from two different verbs). It is also used in the passive voice, and as an adjective, e.g. *I have **broken** the window. The window was **broken**. It's a **broken** window.*

phrase   a group of words which together have some meaning, e.g. *in the square, after midday.*

possessives   words showing ownership or possession, e.g. *my car, it's ours.*

prefix   a number of letters which, when added to the beginning of a word, change its meaning in some way, e.g. *possible – impossible, kind – unkind.*

prepositions   these are words which denote the 'position' of someone or something in time or space, e.g. ***on top of** the cupboard, **in front of** the cinema, **at** six o'clock.*

pronouns   these are words which take the place of a noun (*pro* = for), so that you do not need to keep repeating the actual noun itself each time you want to refer to it. There are various types of pronoun in Portuguese, all of which you will learn about, e.g. *Mary is very kind. **She** looks after my cat. **She** gives **it** lots of treats.*

reflexive verbs   verbs expressing actions with a bearing on the subject. The action is carried out by, and also on, the subject of the verb, i.e. the verb **reflects** back to the person carrying out the action. In English, reflexive verbs carry the word *self* with them. A number of verbs are reflexive in Portuguese but not in English. e.g. *Enjoy yourselves!   She gets herself dressed each morning.*

sentence   a group of words, with a beginning, an end and a finite **verb** (see below), which has a meaning. A sentence may have any number of separate clauses, but one of these will be the main clause, which can make sense in its own right as a sentence. e.g. *She wants to visit America.   If you go there, you must not drink the water.*

stem   the part of a verb to which you add the endings to show person and tense.

subject   the person or thing carrying out the action of a verb. e.g. ***My brother** wants to be a teacher.   **Our dog** always chases spiders.*

subjunctive mood   a separate set of verb endings for use in certain situations, such as in *if* clauses, or with expressions of doubt.

suffix   a letter or letters which, when added to the end of a word, change the meaning or the type of word it is grammatically, e.g. *sad – sadness, glad – gladly.*

superlative   the form of an adjective or adverb denoting the highest or lowest level, e.g. *the fastest car, the trendiest shoes*.

syllable   this is a part of a word containing one, two or more letters which are clumped together so that we can divide up the word as we say it. e.g. *cho-co-late, mag-ni-fi-cent*.

tag question   short question–expressions which, when 'tagged' on to the end of a sentence, turn it into a question, e.g. *It's turned out nice, hasn't it?*

tenses   these are the time references for when actions (verbs) are taking place. There are different tenses in the present, past and future – you will learn what these are in Portuguese. Some of them have different names in Portuguese grammar to what they might be termed in English. Don't worry too much about the actual terminology – concentrate on learning which verb endings to use in what circumstances. e.g. *She **had not wanted** to go to the party.   **Will we have saved** enough money?*

verbs   verbs convey actions or states of being, or sometimes an abstract state. Verbs have an 'infinitive' form, which gives you the name of the verb itself, but no other information – it is the form you will find in the dictionary, and relates to the English *to do something*. A sentence must have a verb in a 'finite' form – which tells you what the action is, who is doing it, and at what point in time (in the past, present or future). English does not change many of its verb endings, but Portuguese, as many languages, has different endings for the person doing the action, and the time, or tense. e.g. *She **goes** home at 5 o'clock. I **watched** TV last night.*

voice   the way you can turn a sentence round and say the same thing in a slightly different way, sometimes for emphasis, e.g. *Our cat chases the dog* (active voice) / *The dog is chased by our cat* (passive voice).

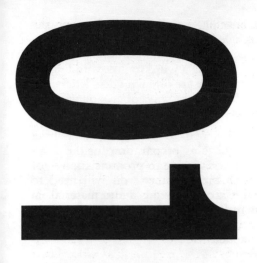

01

Portuguese spelling, accents and stress

In this unit you will learn
- the basics of Portuguese spelling and punctuation
- about accents and stress in Portuguese
- some differences between European and Brazilian Portuguese spelling and use of accents

It is said that Portuguese is a 'phonetic language', i.e. you say something the way it looks. Most experts agree that once you have learned the basics of spelling and pronunciation, you should be able to have a good stab at saying a word (unlike with English or French, for example, where there are often 'hidden' letters and sounds, or where there may be different ways of pronouncing the same letters – think of words in English ending in -*ough*).

This introductory unit is designed to give you some brief guidance on the written language as preparation for the work you will do in the book. It is not a guide to pronunciation – for assistance on how to speak the language you will need to purchase a coursebook with accompanying audio material, in either European or Brazilian Portuguese (see the suggestions in the **Taking it further** section on page 272). There are no exercises with this reference unit.

Spelling

Portuguese uses the Roman alphabet, as do English and other Latin-based languages. However, the letters **k**, **w** and **y** do not naturally occur in Portuguese words – only in imported foreign words and in abbreviations for weights, measures and chemicals, e.g. 10 kg (= 10 **quilos**).

- The only double consonants you will find are **rr** and **ss**.
- There are three extra 'sounds' or letter combinations you will come across a lot: **ch**, **lh**, **nh**. They are known as *diágrafos* – two letters with one sound. For readers with a background in Spanish, **lh** is similar in sound to Spanish **ll**, and **nh** is like **ñ**. **ch** is pronounced *sh* and not *ch* as in Spanish.
- **h** is always silent in Portuguese, thus sometimes making it difficult when listening to discern whether a word begins with a vowel or an **h**. As any dictionary will illustrate, there are in fact a number of words starting with **h**, so learning obvious ones will help – and many are similar to English so you can train yourself to think logically when listening, e.g. **o Otel Miramar** or **o Hotel Miramar?**
- A quick note about the consonants **c**, **g** and **q**, which change their pronunciation depending on which vowels follow them. This can be a stumbling block for the uninitiated, hence some basic rules here:

  c before a / o / u = hard sound, like *cat*

  ç (c + cedilla – see section on accents) before a / o / u = soft sound, like *face* c before e / i = soft

g before e / i = soft, like the s sound in *treasure*

g before a / o / u = hard, like in *goal*

g + u before e / i = 'silent' u , e.g. **guitarra** [ghee... not gwee...]. There are some exceptions (there always are!), such as **linguiça** (*spicy sausage*) [lingwiça].

q is always followed by u.

qu before e / i = 'silent' u, e.g. **máquina** (*machine*) [mákeena **not** mákweena]; again there are some exceptions (e.g. **cinquenta** (*fifty*) (EP) [cinkwenta]).

qu before o / a = kw, e.g. **quadro** (*picture*) [kwadro]

- **ph** does not exist in Portuguese; those words similar to English have an **f** – the same sound, but be careful with the spelling: e.g. **filósofo** = *philosopher*

Brazilian spelling

Despite many years of wrangling over spelling throughout the Portuguese-speaking world (and most particularly between Portugal and Brazil), up-to-date orthographic (spelling) agreements have still not been fully implemented. There are still some differences in spelling between the two main variants of the language, mostly in the following areas, but even these differences are not always applied consistently:

Common changes in consonants from European (EP) to Brazilian (BP) Portuguese

Spelling in EP	Example (EP)	Spelling in BP	Example (BP)
Words with a **b** in the middle	*subtil*	Lose the **b**	*sutil*
cc and cç	*secção*	Lose the first c	*seção*
mm, mn, nn	*connosco* *comummente* *indemnizar*	Become single **n** or **m**	*conosco* *comumente* *indenizar*
pç and pt	*óptimo*	Lose the **p**	*ótimo*
ct	*facto*	Lose the **c**	*fato*
t	*registo*	Become **tr**	*registro*
gu / qu	*cinquenta*	Become **gü / qü**	*cinqüenta*
Numbers 16–19	*dezasseis*	Change **a** to **e**	*dezesseis*

Be careful when using dictionaries – many of the bilingual editions available from UK and US publishers take Brazilian Portuguese as the standard and give that as the first word in an example, if there is a discrepancy between the two, with EP next. They usually put BP or PT after the word, and some, like the larger *Collins*, remind you of some common spelling changes at the foot of each page. Nevertheless, you still need to be on the ball to remember to look out for the differences – many of my own students end up using Brazilian words when they may never set foot in South America! If you can, eventually aim to work with a monolingual dictionary bought either in Portugal or Brazil, alongside your usual one. This will also help you improve your range of vocabulary.

Further information on the differences in written accents follows next, while differences in grammar are pointed out where relevant in each unit, and some common differences in vocabulary are listed on page 261.

Punctuation / *Pontuação*

Just for reference, here are the names of some of the more common features of punctuation – they are useful in dictation!

.	ponto final	!	ponto de exclamação
,	vírgula	...	reticências
;	ponto e vírgula	«...» or "..."	aspas / vírgulas altas (comas)
:	dois pontos	( )	parênteses
?	ponto de interrogação	–	travessão

Students of Spanish should note that Portuguese does not have an upside-down ? or ! at the start of sentences.

Accents

You will find the following written accents in Portuguese:

´	acute accent	*acento agudo*	opens vowel sound and indicates stress*	*gramática*
^	circumflex	*circunflexo*	closes vowel sound and indicates stress	*português*
~	tilde	*til*	nasalizes vowel and usually indicates stress	*amanhã*
`	grave accent	*acento grave*	opens vowel, non-stressing, indicates a contraction of two words: preposition *a* and feminine forms of the definite article and the demonstrative pronouns and adjectives	*àquele*

* Stress is the part of the word you emphasize when you say it.

There are also: ç, cedilha (*cedilla*), which makes the c soft, and, as mentioned previously, the 'dieresis' , ü, in **gü** and **qü**, to show they are pronounced as **gw** and **qw** in Brazilian Portuguese.

Differences in Brazilian Portuguese

Some common changes to written accents are:

European	Brazilian
voo [no accent]	*vôo* [adds circumflex]
ténis [acute **e** accent]	*tênis* [becomes **e** circumflex]
abdómen [acute **o**]	*abdômen* [becomes **o** circumflex]
ideia [no accent]	*idéia* [adds acute accent] – see also Unit 25

Stress

Portuguese words are classified into three groups in terms of where the stress (emphasis) falls:

1 = last syllable
2 = penultimate (next to last) syllable
3 = antepenultimate syllable

The majority belong to group 2 and do not usually require a written accent. The written accent occurs to enable words to be correctly stressed when they have deviated from the usual stress pattern. Whenever you see a written accent, that is where you should emphasize the word when you say it. Words also carry a written stress mark to distinguish them from a word with the same spelling but a different meaning, e.g. **por** (*by*) and **pôr** (*to put*).

The above is a very basic guide to the concept of stress; for a fuller treatment of all the rules refer to the pronunciation guides in courses and dictionaries, and listen to how words are said when you are in a Portuguese-speaking country. The best way to learn how to write the words correctly, though, is by practice, and that includes reading in the language and spotting spellings, as well as noting down new words as you acquire them. So, on with the rest of the book to do just that...

02

nouns and articles

In this unit you will learn
- about masculine and feminine words in Portuguese
- how to form plurals
- the words for *the* (the definite article) and *a, an, some* (the indefinite article) and their uses in Portuguese

Grammar in focus

Gender

All nouns (things, people, places) in Portuguese are grouped into either masculine or feminine words. The so-called 'gender' of words denoting people or animals is determined by their obvious sex.

o senhor	*man, gentleman*	a senhora	*woman, lady*
o touro	*bull*	a vaca	*cow*

Usually, words ending in -o are masculine, and those ending in -a are feminine.

o vestido	*dress*	a casa	*house*
o relógio	*clock*	a janela	*window*

Many nouns become feminine by changing the final -o to -a, or by adding -a to the existing masculine form.

o amigo	*(male) friend*	a amiga	*(female) friend*
o filho	*son*	a filha	*daughter*
o professor	*(male) teacher*	a professora	*(female) teacher*

However, not all nouns fit comfortably into these categories. Words of Greek origin, for example, end in -a but are, in fact, masculine, and there are many other exceptions.

o drama	*drama*	o telegrama	*telegram*
o chá	*tea*	o cinema	*cinema*

Nouns ending in -l and -r are generally masculine, while those ending with the letters -ade, -ção, and -gem are generally feminine.

o jornal	*newspaper*
o favor	*favour*
a caridade	*charity*
a estação	*station*
a estalagem	*inn*

As gender is not always obvious from the ending of a word, nouns should be learned together with the appropriate article. You can check this in your dictionary, where nouns have an *m.* or *f.* after them – unless they fit the normal -o / -a ending pattern, in which case you will not find reference to the gender.

Number

The plural (i.e. when there is more than one) of nouns ending in a vowel is formed by simply adding -s.

a casa	*house*	as casas	*houses*
o carro	*car*	os carros	*cars*
a cidade	*city*	as cidades	*cities*

The plural of nouns ending in a consonant other than -l or -m is formed by adding -es.

a mulher	*woman*	as mulheres	*women*
o cartaz	*poster*	os cartazes	*posters*

Words ending in -m form their plural by changing the -m to -ns.

o homem	*man*	os homens	*men*
a viagem	*journey*	as viagens	*journeys*

Words ending in -l change the -l to -is. If the word ends in -il, this changes to -is if the final syllable is stressed, but changes to -eis if the syllable is unstressed.

o jornal	*newspaper*	os jornais	*newspapers*
o hotel	*hotel*	os hotéis	*hotels*
o ardil	*trick, ruse*	os ardis	*tricks, ruses*
o réptil	*reptile*	os répteis	*reptiles*

Words ending in -ão either add a final -s or change to -ões or -ães; the correct plurals can only be learned through memorization, as there is no standard rule.

o irmão	*brother*	os irmãos	*brothers*
a estação	*station*	as estações	*stations*
o pão	*bread*	os pães	*loaves*

The masculine plural form is used to denote a group of mixed gender.

o pai	*father*	os pais	*parents*
o filho	*son*	os filhos	*sons / children*
o neto	*grandson*	os netos	*grandsons / grandchildren*

Abstract nouns formed from or followed by an adjective are neuter (they have neither masculine nor feminine gender), and therefore do not change in any way.

o importante	*the important thing / what is important...*
o interessante	*the interesting thing / what is interesting...*

Articles

Articles are the words for *the* (definite article) and *a, an, some* (indefinite article). They agree with the noun in both number and gender.

	Singular	Plural
Definite article: 'the'		
(*m.*)	o	os
(*f.*)	a	as
Indefinite article: *a, an, some*		
(*m.*)	um	uns
(*f.*)	uma	umas

The masculine plurals of both articles are used to describe mixed groups of males and females, as well as all-male groups. Even if you happen to have a group of 15 women and two men, the masculine plural **os senhores** would be used to describe the group!

Singular		Plural	
o livro	*the book*	os livros	*the books*
a caneta	*the pen*	as canetas	*the pens*
um carro	*a car*	uns carros	*some cars*
uma blusa	*a blouse*	umas blusas	*some blouses*

Uses of the definite article

Portuguese uses the definite article differently from English in the following situations:

- With titles and first names, and in certain forms of address.

  O doutor Pereira é muito simpático.   *Doctor Pereira is very kind.*

  O Pedro não gosta de peixe.   *Pedro doesn't like fish.*

  A senhora dona Ana Maria trabalha num banco.   *Ana Maria works in a bank.*

- With continents, provinces, and countries (except Portugal, Angola, Mozambique, Cape Verde and several others).

  A África é muito quente.   *Africa is very hot.*

  A Beira Baixa é uma região em Portugal.   *Beira Baixa is a region in Portugal.*

Este ano vamos visitar
  a Espanha.

We're going to visit Spain this year.

- With names of towns that have an actual meaning.

A minha tia mora *no Porto.*   *My aunt lives in Oporto.*
  (o porto = *the port*)
O *Rio* tem um carnaval   *Rio has a great carnival.*
  magnífico. (o rio = *the river*)

- With body parts and clothing, instead of possessive adjectives.

Parti o **braço.**   *I broke my arm.*
Vou pôr o **casaco.**   *I'm going to put my coat on.*
Ela está a lavar os **cabelos.**   *She's washing her hair.*

- With nouns used in a general sense.

As crianças gostam de brincar.   *Children like playing.*
A chuva faz bem **às plantas.**   *Rain is good for plants.*

- With names of languages.

O **chinês** é uma língua   *Chinese is a language spoken*
  falada por milhões.   *by millions.*
Podemos estudar o **espanhol**   *We can study Spanish and*
  e o **francês.**   *French.*

However, the definite article with languages is omitted after **de** or **em,** and may not necessarily follow the verbs **aprender, ensinar, entender, estudar, falar** and **saber.**

O João estuda alemão.   *John studies German.*
Eu falo um pouco de russo.   *I speak a bit of Russian.*

- With units of measurement.

O café custa 4 euros o **quilo.**   *Coffee costs 4 euros a kilo.*
A seda é muito cara: paguei   *Silk is very expensive: I paid*
  8 dólares o **metro.**   *8 dollars a metre.*

- With meals.

Tomo o **pequeno almoço**   *I have breakfast in the*
  na cantina.   *canteen.*
Preparei um frango para   *I prepared a chicken for*
  o **jantar.**   *dinner.*

- With certain public institutions

A minha filha foi **ao**   *My daughter went to (the)*
  hospital.   *hospital.*
Vamos para **a cidade.**   *Let's go to town.*

Omission of articles

Indefinite article

The indefinite article is omitted under these circumstances:

- Before unqualified nouns denoting nationality, rank or profession.

Sou japonês.	*I am (a) Japanese (man).*
O meu irmão é general.	*My brother is a general.*
A Maria é advogada.	*Mary is a lawyer.*

- Before nouns 'in apposition' (with the same function in the sentence), when the noun is not modified.

Cheguei cansada ao meu destino – **Elvas, cidade** do Alentejo, perto da fronteira espanhola.	*I arrived tired at my destination – Elvas, a city in the Alentejo near the Spanish border.*

- Often when the following words are used:

cem	*hundred*	que...!	*what (a)...!*
mil	*thousand*	certo	*certain*
meio	*half*	outro	*other*
semelhante	*such*	tal	*such (a)*

Pedimos outra garrafa de vinho tinto.	*We ordered another bottle of red wine.*
Ganhei mil libras.	*I won a thousand pounds.*
Nunca vimos semelhante coisa!	*We have never seen such a thing!*

Definite article

The definite article is omitted:

- With nouns in apposition, except when the noun is followed by an adjective in the superlative.

Fomos a **Lisboa, capital** do país.	*We went to Lisbon, the capital of the country.*
Lisboa, **a maior** cidade de Portugal, é também a capital.	*Lisbon, the largest city in Portugal, is also the capital.*

- Before a numeral used with the name of a ruler.

João I (primeiro)	*John the First*
Pedro II (segundo)	*Peter the Second*

Neuter article, o

The neuter article originates from Latin, which in fact employed three genders: masculine, feminine, and neuter. It is used with masculine singular adjectives to express the abstract, or general, quality of the adjective. In English, the word *thing* often accompanies the adjective.

O **importante** é que
  compremos já.

*The important thing is that
  we buy now.*

É sempre o **mesmo** com elas.

*It's always the same (thing)
  with them.*

Noun ellipsis

The definite article can be used before **que** or **de** as a demonstrative pronoun.

Os que querem peixe, pois
  que digam!

Those who want fish, say so!

Este é o carro do Pedro,
  e este o do Miguel.

*This is Peter's car, and this
  one is Michael's.*

Neuter o is used when no direct reference to a noun is given.

Não consigo ouvir o que
  estão a dizer.

*I can't hear what they're
  saying.*

Exercises

A Decide whether the following nouns are masculine or feminine, and insert the correct definite article in **1–5**, and the correct indefinite article in **6–10**. You may need to check what some of the words mean in a dictionary, but the meanings are also given in the **Key** to the exercises.

1 .... livro
2 .... senhor
3 .... mesa
4 .... país
5 .... mãe

6 .... restaurante
7 .... informação
8 .... garagem
9 .... café
10 .... cidade

B Plurals of nouns: find eight plural nouns on the wordsearch grid, which correspond to the following singulars:

1 casa
2 país
3 jardim
4 túnel

5 mão
6 tio
7 rapaz
8 jovem

J	A	B	C	T	D	E	F	G	P
O	A	H	I	Ú	J	K	L	M	A
V	N	R	O	M	P	Q	R	S	Í
E	T	A	D	E	U	T	I	O	S
N	V	P	X	I	Y	Z	B	D	E
S	F	A	H	S	N	J	L	N	S
P	R	Z	T	V	X	S	Z	C	E
S	I	E	N	Ú	T	O	R	T	V
X	Z	S	D	F	H	Ã	J	L	N
C	A	S	A	S	T	M	V	X	Z

C Decide whether an article is required in these examples, and if so, insert the most appropriate in each one.

1 .... Nuno é (*is*) muito grande.
2 Tenho (*I have*) .... casa bonita.
3 Sou .... professor.
4 Vamos visitar .... França.
5 O Rei D. Manuel .... primeiro.
6 Queremos (*we want*) .... meia garrafa de vinho.
7 .... japonês é uma língua difícil.
8 .... cigarros fazem mal.

Grammar in context

Look at this shopping list and with help from the vocabulary box, find:

1 three masculine singular products listed
2 how many tomatoes are wanted
3 what would have been written if only one loaf of bread was required

Lista de Compras

um pacote de manteiga
umas laranjas
três pães
meio quilo de tomates
cem folhas de papel
um frango para o almoço
um jornal
um dicionário
uma prenda para a Ana

manteiga	*butter*
laranjas	*oranges*
folhas	*sheets*
o almoço	*lunch*
uma prenda	*a gift*
para	*for*

03

adjectives

In this unit you will learn
- how to make adjectives agree with the words they describe
- about the position of adjectives
- some common Portuguese adjectives

Grammar in focus

Agreement

Adjectives are words which describe, or give additional information about, nouns and pronouns. They agree (have equivalent endings) with the noun in number and gender. If an adjective modifies (describes) two or more nouns of different gender, then it is placed in the masculine plural.

o carro amarelo	*the yellow car*
a porta vermelha	*the red door*
os rapazes bonitos	*the good-looking boys*
as casas antigas	*the old houses*
O quadro é caro.	*The picture is expensive.*
A casa é pequena.	*The house is small.*
Os meninos são altos.	*The boys are tall.*
As flores são lindas.	*The flowers are pretty.*
O Miguel e a irmã são ricos.	*Miguel and his sister are rich.*

Gender

Like nouns, adjectives are masculine or feminine, depending on the noun they are describing. In a dictionary or vocabulary list the adjective is always given in the masculine singular. Those ending in **-o** switch to a final **-a** to form the feminine.

o prato redondo	*the round plate*
a mesa redonda	*the round table*

If an adjective ends in **-e** or a **consonant**, the masculine and feminine forms are usually identical, except in adjectives of nationality.

o filme interessante	*the interesting film*
a música interessante	*the interesting music*
o senhor feliz	*the happy man*
a senhora feliz	*the happy woman*
o senhor espanhol	*the Spanish man*
a senhora espanhola	*the Spanish woman*

Other masculine – feminine changes include:

Masculine			Feminine	
-or	sofredor	*suffering*	+ a	sofredora
-ês	chinês	*Chinese*	+ a	chinesa
-u	nu	*nude*	+ a	nua
-eu	europeu	*European*	+ eia	europeia*
-ão	cristão	*Christian*	+ ã	cristã

* [BP = européia]

There are many exceptions to the above-stated rules, which you will pick up as you go along. Make a note of them if you think they are words you may wish to use yourself.

Number

In general, the plurals of adjectives are formed according to the same rules as for nouns.

o médico simpático	*the nice doctor*
os meninos simpáticos	*the nice boys*
a secretária feliz	*the happy secretary*
as filhas felizes	*the happy daughters*
uma história incrível	*an incredible story*
as aventuras incríveis	*the incredible adventures*

Position

Adjectives are usually placed *after* the noun they are describing. They can also be found before the noun; certain adjectives change their meaning in this case.

uma senhora **pobre**	*a poor woman* (not rich)
uma **pobre** senhora	*a poor woman* (pitiful)

Other adjectives which act in this way include:

	Before the noun	After the noun
grande	*great*	*big*
mesmo	*same*	*self*
vários	*several*	*various*

Ela tem um **grande** plano.	*She has a great plan.*
O Pedro **mesmo** comprou a casa.	*Pedro bought the house himself.*
Várias pessoas foram à festa.	*Several people went to the party.*

The following adjectives tend to be used more frequently before the noun, but can be used in either position:

bom	*good*	velho	*old*
mau	*bad*	único	*only*
lindo	*pretty*	próximo	*next*
pequeno	*small*	último	*last*

Este é um **velho** livro.	*This is an old book.*
A **próxima** aula será no sábado.	*The next class will be on Saturday.*

The ordinal numbers (**primeiro**, *first*; **segundo**, *second*, etc.) are also normally placed before the noun.

É a **primeira** rua à esquerda.	*It's the first street on the left.*
Esta é a **segunda** vez que li o livro.	*This is the second time I've read the book.*

Suffixes

Instead of using the word **muito** (*very*) with an adjective, the suffix -**íssimo** can be added to the adjective after the final vowel has been dropped.

lindo	*pretty*	lind**íssimo**	*very pretty*
grande	*big*	grand**íssimo**	*very big, huge*

Another widely used suffix, -**inho**, denotes affection or pity.

bonito	*pretty*	bonit**inho**	*cute, really pretty*
obrigado	*thank you*	obriga**dinho**	*thanks a lot*
coitado	*poor, pitiful*	coita**dinho**	*poor little thing*

These endings follow the general rules for plural and feminine forms. For other examples of suffixes see Unit 12.

A selection of common descriptive adjectives

alto	*tall; high*	gordo	*fat*
amarelo	*yellow*	gostoso	*tasty*
azul	*blue*	largo	*wide, broad*
baixo	*short; low*	magro	*thin*
barulhento	*noisy*	nervoso	*nervous*
branco	*white*	pobre	*poor*
castanho	*brown*	preto	*black*
certo	*right, correct*	rápido	*fast*
difícil	*difficult*	rico	*rich*
duro	*hard*	simpático	*pleasant, nice*
fácil	*easy*	triste	*sad*
feio	*ugly*	verde	*green*
forte	*strong*	vermelho	*red*

Exercises

A Choose an adjective from the box which best describes each picture, but remember to make it agree in number and gender with what is in the picture.

1 um gato

....

2 uma casa

....

3 duas meninas

....

4 dois senhores

....

5 um monstro

....

6 uma senhora

....

pequeno	alto	triste	bonito	velho
redondo	feliz	feroz		

B Colours and nationalities are adjectives – solve the clues to find the correct forms to complete this puzzle.

Across:
1 um americano, dois ....?
3 uma blusa *red*
5 The sister of an **alemão** is an ....
7 *blue* olhos (*eyes*)
9 an Englishman and his language

Down:
2 masculine of **branca**
4 Trees are this colour.
6 plural of **castanho**
8 more than one **espanhol**
10 a feminine **brasileiro**

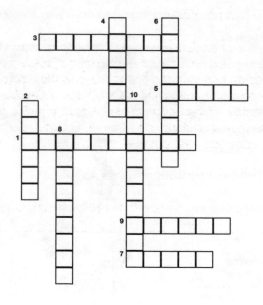

Grammar in context

How many adjectives can you find in a) the singular and b) the plural, in this advert for the Hotel Lusomar?

HOTEL LUSOMAR

6530 Carvoeiro, Algarve, Portugal
Tel: 082 – 657819 / 65720

VISITE O ALGARVE – OFERTA ESPECIAL

Apenas 50 € por pessoa por noite com pequeno almoço

Situado numa posição invejável perto do mar na estância turística de Carvoeiro, o Hotel Lusomar oferece o melhor ambiente de boas-vindas e a nossa cozinha tradicional. O Hotel tem uma magnífica vista do mar e das áreas circundantes, oferecendo acesso directo e fácil à praia, uma das mais populares do Algarve. O Hotel tem uma piscina aquecida e 86 quartos.

Preços válidos até 5 de Abril de 2004

Reserva através dos telefones acima mencionados.

04

adverbs

Grammar in focus

Adverbs are words which provide information about verbs, adjectives and other adverbs. Many of them are equivalent to the English adjective + *-ly*.

Formation

Most adverbs are formed by adding **-mente** to the feminine singular form of the adjective. (If the adjective has only one form for both genders, that form is used.) Accents on the original adjective are dropped.

rápido	*quick*	rapida**mente**	*quickly*
extremo	*extreme*	extrema**mente**	*extremely*
feliz	*happy*	feliz**mente**	*happily*

If two or more adverbs are used in a series of descriptions, **-mente** should be placed only at the end of the last one.

O Alberto compreende
rápida e facilmente.

*Alberto understands quickly
and easily.*

Avoiding the use of *-mente*

To enhance style, and avoid repetition, adverbs ending in **-mente** can be replaced by any of the following:

com + noun *with* ...
duma maneira + adjective *in a ... manner*
dum modo + adjective *in a ... way*

desdenhosamente *scornfully* → com desdém *with scorn*
concentradamente *concentratedly* → duma maneira concentrada
     in a concentrated manner
incrivelmente incredibly → *dum modo incrível* in an incredible way

Adverbs which do not fall into the **-mente** group include:

devagar	*slowly*	bem	*well*
mal	*badly*	cedo	*early*
sempre	*always / still*	depois	*afterwards / later*

Eu sempre gosto de ir
ao teatro.
O Eduardo pinta bem.
A carta chegou uma semana
depois.

*I always like going to the
theatre.*
Eduardo paints well.
The letter arrived a week later.

Often Portuguese uses an adjective in the masculine singular when an adverb would be used in English.

A Sónia canta lindo.   *Sonia sings beautifully.*
Vocês falam baixo.   *You speak quietly.*

Exercises

A Form adverbs from the adjectives in brackets. There is some help with vocabulary in the box below.

1 Está um dia (extremo) quente.

2 Estou (temporário) sem casa.

3 (Final) a música parou.

4 A senhora fala italiano (bom).

5 O tigre corre (rápido).

6 É (real) um bom cantor.

7 Ela trabalha (silencioso).

8 Eles falaram (secreto).

9 O professor falou (franco).

10 É (exacto) [BP = exato] o que penso.

está	*it is*	**quente**	*hot*
estou	*I am*	**sem**	*without*
parou	*stopped*	**corre**	*runs*
cantor	*singer*	**ela trabalha**	*she works*
eles falaram	*they spoke*	**falou**	*spoke*
é	*s/he / it is*	**o que penso**	*what I think*

B Match up the adverbs ending in **-mente** with the correct alternative way of saying the same thing.

1 dificilmente   a com cortesia
2 silenciosamente   b dum modo desconfiado
3 desconfiadamente   c com dificuldade
4 culturalmente   d duma maneira silenciosa
5 cortesmente   e dum modo particular
6 particularmente   f com cultura

Language watch 1

Many Portuguese words ending in **-ção** are equivalent to words in English ending in *-tion*.

a estação   *station*   a infecção   *infection*

Can you guess what these are?

cooperação, protecção, poluição, promoção, comunicação, solução, emoção, decoração

They are all feminine words, and the plural is formed by changing the **-ção** to **-ções**: infecções

Similarly, words ending in **-são** correspond to *-sion* in English

extensão   *extension*   profissão   *profession*
televisão   *television*

Keep an eye out for more examples and add them to your list.

05 comparatives and superlatives

In this unit you will learn

- how to compare adjectives: **feliz, mais feliz, menos feliz** (*happy, happier, less happy*)
- how to form superlatives: **o mais alto, altíssimo** (*the tallest, very tall*)
- ways of expressing equality and inequality (**tão ... como / quanto, mais ... (do) que**)
- about comparing adverbs

Grammar in focus

Adjectives

To form the comparative of an adjective, place **mais** (*more*) or **menos** (*less*) before it. To form the superlative, use the definite article with the comparative. Comparative and superlative adjectives must agree with the nouns they modify.

Adjective	Comparative	Superlative
frio *cold*	**mais** frio *colder*	**o mais** frio *the coldest*
barato *cheap*	**mais** barato *cheaper*	**o mais** barato *the cheapest*
feliz *happy*	**mais** feliz *happier*	**o mais** feliz *the happiest*

A Maria está feliz, mas a Ana está **mais feliz**.

Maria is happy, but Ana is happier.

O Nuno é alto; a Lúmen é mais alta; o Francisco é **o mais alto**.

Nuno is tall; Lúmen is taller; Francisco is the tallest.

Comparatives of inferiority also exist, but are used less:

menos rico *less rich* (i.e. *poorer*) o menos rico *the least rich*

In the superlative, if a noun is included, the definite article should go before it, and both the article and the noun appear before the superlative adjective.

O Miguel é o mais inteligente.

Miguel is the most intelligent.

O Miguel é **o aluno** mais inteligente.

Miguel is the most intelligent pupil.

The article may be used with a possessive, which it precedes.

O Miguel é **o meu** amigo mais inteligente.

Miguel is my most intelligent friend.

De is used to translate *in* after a superlative, and not **em**.

Ela é a menina mais bonita **da** cidade.

She is the prettiest girl in the (= of the) town.

Irregular comparison

Some adjectives have irregular comparatives.

Adjective	Comparative	Superlative
bom *good*	melhor *better*	o melhor; óptimo* *the best*
mau *bad*	pior *worse*	o pior; péssimo *the worst*
grande *big*	maior** *bigger*	o maior; máximo *the biggest*
pequeno *small*	menor** *smaller*	o menor; mínimo *the smallest*

* [BP = ótimo]

** You will also come across **mais grande** and **mais pequeno**.

Alternative absolute superlative adjectives

A bit of a mouthful for an alternative way of expressing superlatives – which is shown below.

baixo *short*   baixíssimo / a *very short / shortest*
fácil *easy*   facilíssimo OR facílimo *really easy / easiest*
tarde *late*   tardíssimo *really late / latest*
grande *large*   grandíssimo OR enorme *huge*

The absolute superlative makes adjectives more intense. To form it, add -íssimo to the last consonant of a basic adjective. There are sometimes spelling or accentuation changes, so it is best to learn these words as you come across them. Some adjectives also have two forms, e.g. **facilíssimo / facílimo**.

Comparison of age

Students with a knowledge of Spanish will know that the irregular comparatives **mayor** and **menor** are used in that language to describe relative age. In Portuguese, **mais velho** (*older*) and **mais novo** (*younger*) are used.

O meu primo é **mais novo** (do) que eu.   *My cousin is younger than me.*

A minha irmã **mais velha** mora na Alemanha.   *My older / eldest sister lives in Germany.*

Levels of comparison

Nouns can be compared in a variety of ways. The word 'than' can be expressed as 'do que' or simply 'que'.

• **Inequality**

do que, que   *than*
mais (do) que   *more ... than*
menos (do) que   *less ... than*

O castelo é mais antigo **do que** a igreja.   *The castle is older than the church.*

Hoje as laranjas estão menos baratas **do que** as maçãs.   *Today the oranges are less cheap than the apples.*

Do que (que) is also used when the clause following the comparison contains a verb.

Nós compramos mais livros **(do) que** vendemos.	*We buy more books than we sell.*

Mais de and **menos de** are used with quantities or numbers.

Tem **menos de** 30 reais.	*He has less than 30 Reais [Brazilian currency].*
Vivi lá **mais de** dez anos.	*I lived there (for) more than ten years.*

• **Equality**

tão + adjective ... como / quanto	*as ... as*
tanto / a + noun ... como	*as much ... as*
tantos / as + noun ... como	*as many ... as*

Sou **tão trabalhador quanto** ela.	*I'm as hard-working as her.*
Ela come **tantos legumes como** frutas.	*She eats as many vegetables as fruit.*

• **Ratio**

quanto mais ... (tanto) mais	*the more ... the more*
quanto mais ... (tanto) menos	*the more ... the less*
quanto menos ... (tanto) mais	*the less ... the more*
quanto menos ... (tanto) menos	*the less ... the less*

Quanto mais cigarros fuma, tanto mais quer.	*The more cigarettes he smokes, the more he wants.*
Quanto maior o prémio, menos felizes estão os que perdem.	*The bigger the prize, the less happy are the losers.*

Adverbs

Comparative adverbs are formed in the same way as comparative adjectives, by using **mais** or **menos**. The superlative also follows the same pattern as for adjectives.

O Miguel corre rapidamente.	*Miguel runs quickly.*
O Pedro corre **mais** rapidamente.	*Pedro runs more quickly.*
O Pedro corre **mais** rapidamente **do que** o Miguel.	*Pedro runs more quickly than Miguel.*
O Paulo corre **o mais** rapidamente.	*Paulo runs the quickest.*

o mais ... possível		*as ... as possible*
o **mais** devagar **possível**		*as slowly as possible*
o **mais** imediatamente possível		*as quickly (immediately) as possible*

Irregular comparisons

bem *well*	melhor *better*	o melhor *the best*
mal *badly*	pior *worse*	o pior *the worst*

Eu canto **bem,** mas a minha irmã canta **melhor.**

I sing well, but my sister sings better.

Ela patina **pior do que** a Carolina.

She skates worse than Carolina (does).

Exercises

A Choose the correct alternative in each sentence to compare different things.

1 O Brasil é maior / menor do que a Inglaterra.
2 Um Ferrari é menos caro / mais caro do que um Ford.
3 A Finlândia é menos fria que / tão fria como a Rússia.
4 Um homem pode correr mais rapidamente / menos rapidamente do que um carro.
5 26 euros são mais de / menos de 35 euros.

B Look at the pictures and decide whether each statement is True or False.

1 A é o mais alto. T/F

2 B é o mais caro. T/F

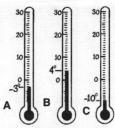

3 C é o menos frio.   T/F

4 B é o mais cedo.   T/F

5 C é o mais pequeno.   T/F

6 A é o mais gordo.   T/F

C Form the correct absolute superlative, meaning *very very…* .

1 É muito **tarde**. É ....

2 Ela é muito **gorda**. Ela é ....

3 As malas estão muito **pesadas**. As malas estão ....

4 Foi (*it was*) um incêndio muito **grave**. Foi um incêndio ....

5 Não é um exame muito **difícil**. Não é um exame ....

6 Os carros são muito **caros**. Os carros são ....

Grammar in context

Why might you want to try the Italian food in this restaurant in Bahia, northern Brazil?

A comida italiana é mais gostosa na Bahia

CANTINA ITALIANÍSSIMA
Cozinha Italiana e Internacional

Rua da Sé, 246, Salvador. Fone: 321–600–1853

06

demonstrative adjectives and pronouns

In this unit you will learn
• how to point things and people out with demonstrative adjectives and pronouns

Grammar in focus

Demonstrative adjectives

Demonstrative adjectives are used to point out or indicate something or someone. As adjectives, they agree with the noun in number and gender, but unlike other adjectives, demonstratives always precede the noun.

Singular		Plural	
este (m.)	} *this*	estes (m.)	} *these*
esta (f.)		estas (f.)	
esse (m.)	} *that*	esses (m.)	} *those*
essa (f.)		essas (f.)	
aquele (m.)	} *that*	aqueles (m.)	} *those*
aquela (f.)		aquelas (f.)	

There are two ways of expressing *that*: **esse** (**essa** etc.), used to refer to objects near to the person being addressed, and **aquele** (**aquela** etc.), for objects at a distance from both the person being addressed and the person talking.

esta flor   essa flor   aquela flor

este livro	*this book*
essa cadeira	*that chair (near you)*
aquele carro na rua	*that car in the street*
Estes hotéis são caros.	*These hotels are expensive.*
Aquelas casas lá são novas.	*Those houses (over) there are new.*

Demonstrative pronouns

These are identical in form to the demonstrative adjectives above. Additionally, there is a singular, neuter pronoun, which is used to refer to abstract concepts and indefinable objects. The demonstrative pronouns take the place of nouns, and often are translated as *this one*, or *that one*.

Singular		Plural	
este (m.)	} this; this one	estes (m.)	} these
esta (f.)		estas (f.)	
isto (n.)	this (thing)		
esse (m.)	} that; that one	esses (m.)	} those
essa (f.)		essas (f.)	
isso (n.)	that (thing)		
aquele (m.)	} that; that one	aqueles (m.)	} those
aquela (f.)		aquelas (f.)	
aquilo (n.)	that (thing)		

The three neuter demonstratives are invariable – they never change their endings, even when referring to something in the plural, e.g. **O que é aquilo? Aquilo são papéis.** *What's that? That (they) are papers.* This means that the invariable demonstratives can be used with both **é** (*is*) and **são** (*are*), the verb depending on the item(s).

The placing adverbs **aqui** (*here*), **aí** (*there*, near the person being addressed), and **ali** (*there*, away from both parties) are often used with demonstratives.

Este quadro e **aquele** azulejo **ali** são muito antigos.	*This painting and that azulejo tile over there are very old.*
De quem são **estes** óculos?	*Whose glasses are these?*
Estes são da Ana.	*These are Ana's.*
Que é **isto**?	*What is this?*
O que é **isso** que tem no chapéu?	*What's that (thing) you've got on your hat?*

The appropriate forms of **este** and **aquele** can be used to denote *the former* (**aquele**) and *the latter* (**este**).

O Rio e Manaus são cidades no Brasil; **esta** fica no norte, **aquela** no sul.   *Rio and Manaus are cities in Brazil; the latter is in the north, the former in the south.*

In this example, Manaus is the city nearer to the end of the phrase (at the semicolon), and so is referred to as **esta**; O Rio is

further away from the end of the phrase, and so is referred to as
aquela.

O João e o Paulo são irmãos; este tem 10 anos e aquele 12.
*João and Paulo are brothers; the latter is 10 years old and the
former is 12.*

Exercises

A Choose the correct form of **este, esse** or **aquele** to fill in the
blanks. Look carefully for clues as to which demonstrative to
use in each case.

1 .... flores aqui	**6** .... sapatos ali
2 .... carro aí	**7** .... café aqui
3 .... casa ali	**8** .... pessoas aí
4 .... bolos aí	**9** .... senhor ali
5 .... senhora aqui	**10** .... livros aqui

B Translate the following:

1 What is this (thing)?
2 That (thing) [near the person addressed] is a book.
3 these ladies here
4 that hat over there
5 Aquilo é um dicionário.
6 Isto aqui são óculos.
7 Esse bolo é de amêndoa (*almond*).
8 Salvador e Campinas são cidades no Brasil; esta fica no sul,
aquela no norte.

Grammar in context

Read this dialogue in a clothes shop and spot the
demonstratives. Make a note of each one you find and work out
what they all mean. The vocabulary box will help you
understand what's going on.

Customer	Bom dia. Posso ver aquela blusa verde?
Shop Asst.	Com certeza. Esta é muito bonita. Gosta?
Customer	Gosto, sim, mas tem uma em azul?
Shop Asst.	Tenho. Veja, estas aqui também são bonitas.
Customer	Sim, são. Prefiro essa que tem aí. O que é aquilo ali?

Shop Asst.	Aquilo são saias curtas. Quer ver?
Customer	Hoje não, obrigada. Levo só esta blusa.

Posso ver?	*Can I see?*
saias curtas	*short skirts*
com certeza	*of course*
Quer ver?	*Do you want to see?*
Gosta? / Gosto.	*Do you like (it)? / I like (it).*
hoje	*today*
tem / tenho	*you have / I have*
levo	*I'll take*
Veja	*Look*
só	*only, just*
também	*also, too*

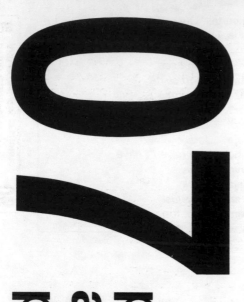

07

possessive adjectives and pronouns

In this unit you will learn
- how to talk about possession in Portuguese with adjectives and pronouns (*my / mine, your / yours,* etc.)

Grammar in focus

The possessive pronouns and their corresponding adjectives are identical in form, and both agree in number and gender with the thing possessed, not the possessor. They are both preceded by the definite article, although it often tends to be dropped when using the pronoun. Brazilian Portuguese often omits the article with both pronoun and adjective.

Possessive adjectives

	Singular		Plural	
	Masculine	Feminine	Masculine	Feminine
my	o meu	a minha	os meus	as minhas
your (familiar)*	o teu	a tua	os teus	as tuas
his / her / your (formal)*	o seu	a sua	os seus	as suas
our	o nosso	a nossa	os nossos	as nossas
your (familiar)*	o vosso	a vossa	os vossos	as vossas
their / your (formal)*	o seu	a sua	os seus	as suas

*For more details on forms of address ('you' forms), see Unit 17.

o meu amigo	*my (male) friend*
a tua mala	*your suitcase*
os seus jornais	*his / her / your / their newspapers*
as nossas chaves	*our keys*
o vosso relógio	*your watch / clock* (addressing *vocês*)
a sua escola	*her / his / your / their school*

O(s) **seu(s)** and a(s) **sua(s)** can be ambiguous, as they have a variety of meanings. In order to avoid confusion, the following forms are often used after the noun to mean *his, her, their*:

dele	*of him (his)*
dela	*of her (her)*
deles	*of them* (m.) *(their)*
delas	*of them* (f.) *(their)*
as canetas **dele**	*his pens* (i.e. the pens of him)
o pai **delas**	*their father* (i.e. the father of them)
as revistas **dela**	*her magazines* (i.e. the magazines of her)

Possessive adjectives are used less in Portuguese than in English, especially with parts of the body and clothing which belong to the subject of the verb, and when the possession is obvious. Instead, the definite article is used on its own.

Cortei o dedo.	*I cut my finger.*
Vou pôr as luvas.	*I'm going to put my gloves on.*
O que tem no saco?	*What have you got in your bag?*

Possessive pronouns

The forms for possessive pronouns are identical to those for the adjectives. The definite article tends to be omitted after forms of the verb *to be*, **ser**. The pronouns agree with the thing possessed. These pronouns take the place of nouns, and are equivalent to the English *mine, yours, his, hers, its, ours* and *theirs*.

A minha é boa.	*Mine is good.*
Os nossos estão no armário.	*Ours are in the wardrobe / cupboard.*
Esse vestido não é **teu**.	*That dress isn't yours.*
De quem é este chocolate?	*Whose chocolate is this?*
É **meu**.	*It's mine.*

To avoid ambiguity in the third person forms, the following forms are often used:

O / a / os / as dele	*his*
O / a / os / as dela	*hers*
O / a / os / as deles	*theirs* (m.)
O / a / os / as delas	*theirs* (f.)

O nosso apartamento é novo, mas o deles é velho.   *Our apartment is new, but theirs is old.*
A namorada do Paulo era bonita; a dele era feia.   *Paulo's girlfriend was pretty; his was ugly.*
As minhas filhas fazem muito barulho; as deles não.   *My daughters make a lot of noise; theirs don't.*

Exercises

A Complete the table by supplying the correct form of the possessive adjectives on each row.

Masc. singular	Fem. singular	Masc. plural	Fem. plural
o meu irmão	1 .... irmã	2 ...... irmãos	as minhas irmãs
3 ...... médico	a tua professora	4 ...... amigos	as tuas mesas
o seu copo	5 ...... rosa	os seus discos	6 ...... camisolas
7 ...... cão	a nossa casa	8 ...... filhos	as nossas férias
o vosso país	9 ...... sopa	os vossos limões	10 ...... janelas

B Choose the correct form from the three possibilities to answer the questions.

1 De quem é este carro? É ....
  a minha **b** meu **c** meus
2 Ali está a senhora Oliveira com o filho ....
  a dele **b** seu **c** dela
3 Esta é .... casa.
  a o nosso **b** a nossa **c** as nossas
4 De quem são aquelas chaves? São [do João] ....
  a vossas **b** dela **c** dele
5 Tens .... livro contigo?
  a o teu **b** os teus **c** o seu
6 Este livro é ...., Paula?
  a sua **b** seu **c** seus

Grammar in context

Joana is describing a photo of her wedding. Can you work out:

1 the name of Nuno's mother?
2 who Ricardo is?
3 to whom the two little girls belong?
4 who is 85?
5 who lives in Italy?

> Este é o meu marido, Nuno, e os pais dele, a Dona Ana Maria, e o António. Os meus pais chamam-se Eduarda e Ricardo. A minha irmã, Mónica, está cá, mas o marido não. Os nossos avós estão com ela. A nossa avó tem 85 anos. O irmão do meu marido e a esposa vieram também, com as filhas. O meu cunhado chama-se Paulo, e vive na Itália.

08

relative pronouns and adjectives

In this unit you will learn
- how to join clauses (parts of sentences) together with relative pronouns and adjectives

Grammar in focus

Relative pronouns and adjectives are used to join, or relate, a dependent clause to the main clause of a sentence. A dependent clause refers to something or someone previously mentioned (the 'antecedent'). The relative pronoun can be a subject, object, or the object of a preposition. The relative pronouns most commonly used are:

que	*who, whom, which, that*
quem	*who, whom*
o / a qual (os / as quais)	*who, whom, which, that*
o que	*which*

Although in essence they have the same forms as interrogative pronouns (see Unit 11), remember that relatives do **not** ask questions.

Pronouns

Que refers to both people and things, and can be either a subject or an object. Following a preposition it refers only to things.

A senhora **que** trabalha no Turismo é simpática.	*The lady who works in the Tourist Office is nice.*
A senhora **que** vimos no Turismo é portuguesa.	*The lady whom we saw in the Tourist Office is Portuguese.*
Temos um carro velho **que** vamos vender.	*We have an old car that we're going to sell.*
O armário em **que** guardei os papéis está fechado à chave.	*The cupboard in which I stored the papers is locked.*

Quem is used only to refer to people, and follows a preposition.

O senhor **com quem** está a falar é o meu professor.	*The man with whom you are talking is my teacher.*
A amiga **para quem** fiz o bolo faz anos hoje.	*The friend for whom I made the cake has her birthday today.*

Quem can also be used without an antecedent, referring to no specific person (*someone / no one*). See also Unit 44.

Quem estudar muito, aprenderá muito.	*Those who study a lot will learn a lot.*
Procuramos **quem** possa cortar a relva.	*We're looking for someone who can cut the lawn.*
Não há **quem** saiba a resposta.	*There's no one who knows the answer.*

O **qual** can be used in place of **que**, when referring to people, to avoid ambiguity. The definite article agrees in gender and number with the antecedent. Look at the following ambiguous sentence:

Estão a falar com a tia do Paulo, que a minha amiga já conhece.	*They are talking with Paulo's aunt, who my friend already knows.*

It is unclear whether the friend knows Paulo or the aunt. The use of the feminine **a qual** in the following sentence leaves no doubt that this reference is to the aunt.

Estão a falar com a tia do Paulo, **a qual** a minha amiga já conhece.

O **qual** is also used with prepositions, especially compound prepositions (those consisting of more than one word).

Vamos visitar o castelo em torno **do qual** há um grande mistério.	*Let's visit the castle around which is a huge mystery.*
Esta é a casa **na qual** passei a infância.	*This is the house in which (where) I spent my childhood.*

O **que** is a neuter relative used when there is no specific noun as an antecedent. It refers to the preceding phrase or idea as a whole.

Chegaram cedo, **o que** me deu pouco tempo para preparar a comida.	*They arrived early, which left me little time to prepare the food.*
Nunca me diz muito, **o que** me irrita.	*He never tells me much, which annoys me.*

Adjectives

Cujo / -s / -a / -as (*whose, of whom, of which*) is a relative adjective, and as such agrees in gender and number with the thing possessed and is used in the same way as the pronouns.

Este é o meu amigo **cujo** carro é um Mercedes.	*This is my friend whose car is a Mercedes.*
Visitámos o museu **cujas** portas são de prata.	*We visited the museum, the doors of which are made of silver.*

Quanto / -s / -a / as (*all that*) is often used in the place of **todo
o / todos os / tudo o que** etc. (*all of which*).

Deram-me todo o dinheiro que tinham. ⎤ *They gave me all the*
Deram-me **quanto** dinheiro tinham. ⎦ *money they had.*

Gastei tudo o que ganhei. ⎤ *I spent all that I won.*
Gastei **quanto** ganhei. ⎦

Onde (*where*) and its forms **aonde / para onde** (*to where*) and **de
onde / donde** (*from where*) are also used in relative clauses and
sometimes as an alternative to some of the words listed above.

Casou-se na casa **onde** (em   *He got married in the house*
  que / na qual) morava.   *where he used to live.*

Exercises

A Match up the English sentences **1–10** with the Portuguese **a–j**.

1 He likes the house where (in which) he lives.

2 The train on which we travelled didn't have a buffet car.

3 The boy whose eyes are green is Dutch.

4 The cakes that we sell here are all home-made.

5 Maria is a friend who lives near me.

6 The cousin with whom I always go out is going to university.

7 The house, the walls of which are yellow, is horrible.

8 Lisbon is a city in which (where) there is a lot to do.

9 The doctor I spoke to you about is over there.

10 The party to which we were invited is tomorrow.

a Os bolos que vendemos aqui são todos caseiros.

b A casa cujas paredes são amarelas é horrível.

c Gosta da casa onde mora.

d A médica de quem te falei está ali.

e O menino cujos olhos são verdes é holandês.

f O primo com quem sempre saio vai para a universidade.

g Lisboa é uma cidade onde há muito para fazer.

h O comboio [BP=trem] em que viajámos não tinha restaurante.

i A festa para a qual fomos convidados é amanhã.

j A Maria é uma amiga que mora perto da minha casa.

B Substitute the words in *italics* with the correct form of the relative **cujo**. You will also need to insert the verbs **é** (*is*) or **são** (*are*).

e.g. A casa *com o jardim bonito* é a nossa. → A casa cujo jardim é bonito é a nossa.

1 A cidade *com as casas brancas* é muito famosa.
2 O aluno (pupil) *com os melhores resultados* ganha um prémio.
3 As estrelas de ténis [BP = tênis) *com a roupa Nike* são russas.
4 O livro *de capa* (cover) *de couro* (leather) é muito antigo.
5 Aquele senhor *de chapéu azul* é um actor [BP = ator] famoso.

Grammar in context

Which relative pronouns (**onde** or **que**) have been left out of this advert for the Caldeiradas restaurant?

Restaurantes

Caldeiradas
R. José António Rocha, 1 A/B Trafaria
☎ *21 295 7622* ℂ *12h–15h30,*
19h–22h30; 46 lugares P *MB*

• A cerca de oito km da praia vai encontrar este restaurante na vila da Trafaria ... a especialidade é o peixe fresco. Na lista a Cataplana de Peixe, ... pode ser de tamboril, de cherne ou corvina (€21 2 pax), a Caldeirada, confeccionada pelo proprietário e ... representa a casa (€16 2 pax, €9,75 1 pax), o Arroz de Tamboril (€21 2 pax) ou as Massinhas no Caldo, prato ... o cliente escolhe o peixe (€ 9,50/€13) são presença constante.

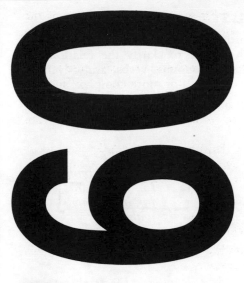

09

prepositions

In this unit you will learn
- simple and compound prepositions in Portuguese (words indicating place, time, etc.)
- some verb + preposition phrases
- how to say when something happens (time / date etc.)
- how to combine prepositions with definite and indefinite articles

Grammar in focus

Prepositions are those words generally indicating place, time, manner and movement that serve to clarify the relationship between other words (nouns, pronouns, verbs, and adverbs). They can be simple, like *em* (*in*, *on*) or more complex, such as *dentro de* (*inside*).

Simple prepositions

a	*at, to*		em	*in, on, at*
antes	*before*		entre	*between, among*
após	*after*		para	*for, to, towards*
até	*up to, until*		por	*for, by, through*
com	*with*		sem	*without*
contra	*against*		sob	*below, under*
de	*of, from, about*		sobre	*on, on top of, about*
desde	*since, from*			

Vou ao mercado.	*I'm going to the market.*
Fui com a minha amiga.	*I went with my friend.*
A padaria é entre o banco e o cinema.	*The baker's is between the bank and the cinema.*
É uma revista sobre férias.	*It's a magazine about holidays.*

For a fuller explanation of **para** and **por** and their differences, see Unit 10.

Compound prepositions

à frente (de)	*at the front (of)*		detrás (de)	*behind*
além (de)	*beyond, besides*		em cima (de)	*on top of*
antes (de)	*before*		em frente (de)	*in front of*
ao redor (de)	*around*		em volta (de)	*around, about*
através (de)	*through, across*		fora (de)	*outside*
atrás (de)	*behind*		longe (de)	*far (from)*
à volta (de)	*around, about*		perto (de)	*near*
debaixo (de)	*under*		por cima (de)	*over, above*
defronte (de)	*opposite*		por dentro (de)	*(from) inside*
dentro (de)	*inside*		por volta (de)	*around, about*
depois (de)	*after*			

The word **de** is used when the preposition is followed by other words (nouns, verbs, pronouns). When it is followed by articles and demonstratives, it combines and contracts with them. See page 51.

A aldeia fica além dos montes.	*The village is beyond the hills.*
O gato está debaixo da mesa.	*The cat is under the table.*

Moramos detrás duma escola.   *We live behind a school.*
O João está lá fora.   *João is out there.*

Verbs with prepositions

As well as those verbs discussed in Unit 24, which take on specific meanings when followed by a preposition, verbs in the infinitive may also be preceded by prepositions.

Além de trabalhar no banco,   *As well as working in a bank,*
    também dá aulas de inglês.   *she also gives English lessons.*
Antes de sair, tenho que   *Before going out I have to*
    limpar a casa.   *clean the house.*
Depois de fazer exercício,   *After doing exercise, it's good*
    é bom beber água.   *to drink water.*

Constructions using a preposition + **que** + verb form what is known as a compound conjunction. These often call for a subjunctive verb form, and may require some practice. See Unit 43.

Paguei as lições de Biologia   *I paid for the Biology lessons*
    para que ela aprendesse   *so that she could learn*
    mais.   *more.*

Prepositions of time

a *at, on*

Used with: dates with a day of the month, time, parts of the day, days of the week (when talking about usual habits)

O dia de Portugal é a 10   *Portugal's National Day is on*
    de Junho.   *the 10th June.*
A loja fecha às sete horas.   *The shop closes at 7 o'clock.*
A festa é à noite.   *The party is at night (in the*
    evening).

Sempre vamos ao clube ao(s)   *We always go to the club on a*
    domingo(s).   *Sunday (on Sundays).*

de *from, of*

Used with: dates, parts of the day, times

A minha data de nascimento   *My date of birth is the 15th of*
    é o dia 15 de Setembro   *September, 1965.*
    [BP = setembro] de 1965.

Não trabalha de manhã. *She doesn't work in the morning.*

O avião parte às 10 horas da noite. *The plane departs at 10 o'clock at night.*

O banco abre das 08.30 às 13.45. *The bank opens from 8.30 until 1.45.*

em *in, on, at*

Used with: dates (with the word *day*), months, (specific) days of the week, years, special festivities, centuries, seasons

O curso termina no dia 10. *The course ends on the 10th.*

Sempre tiramos férias em Março [BP = março]. *We always have holidays in March.*

Na terça(-feira) ela vai ao hospital. *On Tuesday she's going to the hospital.*

A Segunda Guerra Mundial terminou em 1945. *World War II ended in 1945.*

No Natal faz calor no Brasil. *At Christmas it is hot in Brazil.*

Morreu no século XV. *He died in the 15th century.*

Na Primavera está menos frio. *It's not as cold in the Spring.*

Other expressions

antes de *before*

Ela chegou **antes de** mim. *She arrived before me.*

Temos de partir **antes das** sete. *We have to leave before seven.*

à volta de, por volta de, por, lá para [BP] *about, around*

A festa começa **pelas** dez horas. *The party begins around ten.*

Chegamos [BP] **lá para** meia-noite. *We arrived at about midnight.*

depois de, após *after*

A loja abre só **depois do** meio-dia. *The store only opens after noon.*

O calor continuou, semana **após** semana. *The heat continued, week after week.*

desde ... até *from ... until*

Ficámos à espera **desde** as quatro **até** às nove da noite. *We waited from four until nine at night.*

Contraction

The following prepositions combine and contract with definite and indefinite articles and demonstratives.

Preposition	+ def. article	+ indef. article	+ demonstrative
a	ao / à/ aos / às		
em	no / na / nos / nas	num / numa / nuns / numas	neste(s) / nesta(s) / nisto nesse(s) / nessa(s) / nisso naquele(s) / naquela(s) naquilo
de	do / da / dos / das	dum / duma duns / dumas	deste(s) / desta(s) / disto desse(s) / dessa(s) / disso daquele(s) / daquela(s) / daquilo
por	pelo / pela / pelos / pelas		

Fomos à pastelaria.
Mora **num** condomínio.

We went to the cake shop.
She lives in a condominium (housing complex).

Gosto mais **daquele**.
Estão a correr **pelas** ruas.

I like that one best.
They are running through the streets.

Other contractions, such as **de** + **algum** → **dalgum**, exist, but also appear in the written language as two separate words, although usually pronounced as one when spoken. It can be more literary to utilize the uncontracted form.

Exercises

A Decide where the toad (**o sapo**) is in each picture.

1 a árvore

2 o rio

3 uma ponte

4 um balde

5 as flores

6 a pá / a forquilha

7 o barril

8 o lago

B Fill in the blanks by choosing from the prepositions listed in the box.

1 Vou .... cinema.
2 Vou .... nove horas.
3 Este é o comboio .... Faro?
4 O programa começa (starts) às duas .... tarde.
5 Vamos .... táxi?
6 Ela foi (*went*) ao médico .... quinta-feira.
7 Não quero ir .... meu carro.
8 São cinco .... as oito. (07.55)
9 Vai .... esta avenida.
10 Termina lá .... onze horas.

para	da	ao	pelas	às
para	na	por	no	de

Grammar in context

You have picked up a guide to your holiday apartment, but the
text accompanying the diagram overleaf does not match it
properly. Read each statement and find the three incorrect ones.

Bem-vindos ao apartamento Sol do Mar.

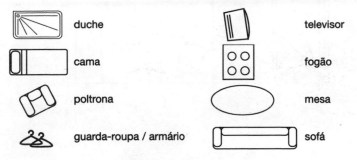

duche

televisor

cama

fogão

poltrona

mesa

guarda-roupa / armário

sofá

1 A casa de banho é à direita do apartamento.
2 Na sala há uma mesa.
3 Há um televisor em cima da mesa.
4 A cozinha tem um fogão no canto.
5 No quarto há uma poltrona entre as camas.
6 A sala é em frente da casa de banho.
7 Há dois sofás à volta da mesa.

bem-vindos	*welcome*	**a cozinha**	*kitchen*
a sala	*living room*	**no canto**	*in the corner*
o quarto	*bedroom*	**à direita**	*on the right*
a casa de banho [BP = banheiro]		*bathroom*	

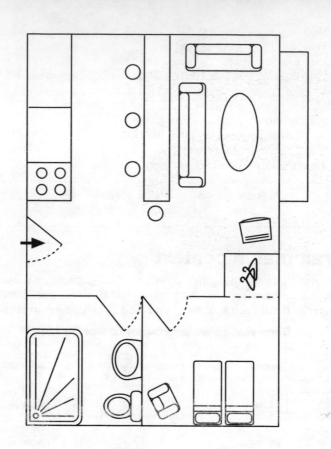

10

por and para

In this unit you will learn
- the prepositions *por* and *para* and their different uses

Grammar in focus

The prepositions **por** and **para** can cause some confusion, as their varied meanings sometimes overlap. **Por** contracts with the definite article to form **pelo / -a / -os / -as**.

Por

Por (*for, through, by, along, per, because of*) is used in the following situations:

- Expressions of place – *through, by, along* or *near which.*

Vamos dar uma volta **pelo** parque.	Let's go for a walk through the park.
O comboio [BP = trem] passa **pela** casa do Paulo.	The train passes near Paulo's house.

- Expressions of time – *through, during, for, around.*

Dançámos **pela** noite inteira.	We danced throughout the whole night.
Fomos ao Canadá **por** dez dias.	We went to Canada for ten days.
Voltámos para casa **pelas** 4 horas.	We returned home around 4 o'clock.

- Exchange, price for, substitution for.

Paguei dois euros **por** um bolo e um café.	I paid 2 euros for a cake and a coffee.
Pode trocar este prato sujo **por** outro?	Can you change this dirty plate for another one?

- Unit of measure (*by / per*), frequency (*per*).

Como se vendem as laranjas? **Por** quilo.	How are the oranges sold? By the kilo.
Quantas vezes por semana compras um jornal?	How many times a week do you buy a paper?

- Way or means by, through which.

Mando o pacote **por** avião.	I'll send the packet by air.
Soubemos do casamento **por** amigos.	We found out about the wedding through friends.

- *Because of, on account of, for.*

Gostei do filme **pela** música e **pela** paisagem.	I liked the film for its music and the scenery.

A região do Douro é conhecida **pelos** bons vinhos.	*The Douro region is well known for its good wines.*

- To go for, send for something.

Foi ao mercado **por** umas pêras.	*He went to the market for some pears.*
Mandou-me ao talho [BP açougue] **por** salsichas.	*She sent me to the butcher's for sausages.*

- On behalf of, for the sake of, for.

Este ano não votei **por** partido nenhum.	*This year I didn't vote for any party.*
Falo **por** todos quando digo...	*I speak for everyone when I say...*

- Motive, reason for.

Levou o dinheiro **por** necessidade.	*He took the money by necessity.*
Morreram todos **por** estupidez.	*They all died through stupidity.*

- On the occasion of.

Não quero prendas **pelo** meu aniversário.	*I don't want presents for my birthday.*

- In the passive voice, to introduce the agent – *by* (see Unit 39).

Eu fui mordida **por** um cão.	*I was bitten by a dog.*
Os carros foram vendidos **pelo** meu irmão.	*The cars were sold by my brother.*

Para

Para (*for, to, in order to, towards*) is used in the following situations:

- Use, *for.*

Este é um CD **para** aprender francês.	*This is a CD for learning French.*
A nova loja vende tudo **para** o desporto [BP = esporte].	*The new shop sells everything for sport.*

- Destination (place or person) towards / for direction

Partiram **para** a Brasília.	*They departed for Brasilia.*

Este bolo não é **para** ti. *This cake is not for you.*
Vamos **para** o sul. *We're going to the south.*

- Purpose, in order to.

Telefono-te **para** combinar *I'll phone you to sort out the*
os detalhes. *details.*
Fui a Londres **para** visitar *I went to London (in order) to*
uma amiga. *visit a friend.*

- Time expressions, *for, by, towards.*

Quero tudo **para** amanhã. *I want it all by tomorrow.*
As férias começam lá **para** *The holidays begin towards*
fins de Julho [BP = julho]. *the end of July.*

- Comparison – *for me, for him* etc.

Isto é muito difícil **para** mim, *This is very difficult for me, but*
mas não **para** eles. *not for them.*

Exercises

A Choose **por** or **para** to fill in the blanks.

1 Amanhã vamos ..PARA.... Coimbra.
2 Comprou uma blusa .POR....... 15 dólares.
3 Este livro é .PARA.... ler durante as férias.
4 Estamos aqui ...PARA... contarmos as novidades.
5 Contei as notas uma ...POR...... uma.
6 A Sílvia foi-se descansar (*to rest*) ...POR...... estar muito
cansada.
7 Este palácio foi construído ...POR.... um engenheiro alemão.
8 Estou a preparar uma festa ..PARA.. as crianças.
9 Deixa-me fazer o trabalho .PARA... ti.
10 Pode limpar o carro ..PARA.... sábado?

B Say whether these sentences have the correct preposition in
them. Answer with 'correct' or 'incorrect'.

1 Gostamos de andar pela praia.
2 Esta é uma caixa para guardar caramelos.
3 Esperei para um momento.
4 Vamos para a Espanha.
5 Pagou 30 euros para o casaco.
6 Quero esta seda por fazer um vestido.

7 Temos um salário de 100 libras por dia.
8 Podem fazer o bolo por amanhã?
9 Entrou por força.
10 O exercício é fácil para ele.

Language watch 2

There are many words starting with **es** + consonant in Portuguese. If you remove the first **e**, you are often much closer to the English word:

escola	→ scola	→ *school*
estação	→ stação	→ *station*
Espanha	→ spanha	→ *Spain*
especial	→ special	→ *special*
espaço	→ spaço	→ *space*
escala	→ scala	→ *scale*

Have a look in the Portuguese part of your dictionary and see how many other words beginning with **es** + consonant become much more familiar in this way.

11

negatives, interrogatives and exclamations

In this unit you will learn
- common negatives in Portuguese, and how to respond negatively to a question
- how to use interrogatives (question words)
- exclamations such as **Que…!** and **Como…!**

Grammar in focus

Negatives

Não (*no, not*) always precedes the verb, but can also follow other words. Portuguese also uses double negatives in the following sequence: **não** + verb + another negative.

Common negatives

não *no, not*

Ela **não** fala italiano.	*She does not speak Italian.*
Já **não** há pão. ?	*There is no bread left.*

nada *nothing (anything)*

Não havia **nada** para fazer.	*There was nothing to do.*
Não gosta de **nada**.	*She does not like anything.*
Nada me apetece.	*Nothing appeals to me.*

ninguém *nobody / no one (anybody / anyone)*

Não apareceu **ninguém**.	*Nobody appeared.*
Não havia **ninguém** em casa.	*There wasn't anyone at home.*
Ninguém comeu.	*Nobody ate.*

nenhum / nenhuma *no, none (any)*

Não há **nenhum** problema.	*There is no problem.*
Não gostou de **nenhum**.	*He didn't like any of them.*
Nenhuma delas falou.	*None of them spoke.*

- The plural forms of **nenhuns** and **nenhumas** are hardly ever used.

- For emphasis, the negative other than **não** can be placed after the noun.

Não tenho carro **nenhum**.	*I don't have a car at all.*

também não *not either, neither*

Eu **não** como carne; o meu marido **também não**.	*I don't eat meat; neither does my husband.*

nem *nor, neither*

Não falamos alemão, **nem** francês.	*We do not speak German or French.*
O João não gosta de fígado. **Nem** eu!	*João does not like liver. Me neither!*

nem ... nem *neither ... nor (any ... or)*

Eles não trouxeram **nem** casaco **nem** luvas.	*They didn't bring a coat or gloves.*
O filho dela não gosta **nem** de jogar futebol, **nem** de nadar.	*Her son doesn't like playing football or swimming.*

nem sequer *not even*

Nem sequer visita a sua mãe.	*You don't even visit your mother.*

nunca *never (ever)*   **jamais** *never (=stronger)*

Vocês **nunca** fazem o trabalho.	*You never do the work.*
Não me telefona **nunca**.	*She never rings me.*
Jamais se esquecerão deste dia.	*They will never forget this day.*

Negative responses

In responding to a question in a negative way, Portuguese tends to use a double negative. Note, too, how the responses often contain a verb, where in English you would not necessarily use one.

Gostas de arroz? **Não, não** gosto.	*Do you like rice? No, I don't (like).*
Quer dar um passeio? **Não** quero, **não**.	*Do you want to go for a stroll? No, I don't (want).*
Este é o autocarro [BP = ônibus] para Santos? **Não, não** é. (or) **Não** é, **não**.	*Is this the bus to Santos? No, it isn't.*

Interrogatives (questions)

To make a question out of a general statement, simply raise the intonation of your voice at the end of the sentence to make it sound like a question.

Foi ao cinema.	*You went to the cinema.*
Foi ao cinema?	*Did you go to the cinema? (lit. You went to the cinema?)*

Interrogatives (question words), such as *who, what, where*, etc., are classified as adjectives, pronouns or adverbs.

Adjectives and pronouns

Que...? / O que...? (particularly in
   conversation)
Quê? / O quê? (when they stand alone
   as a question)
                                          What...? / Which...?

Quem?	*Who?*
A quem?	*To whom?*
Qual, quais?	*What, which ones?*
Quanto / a?	*How much?*
Quantos / as?	*How many?*

O que aconteceu?	*What happened?*
Sabes uma coisa? **O quê?**	*Do you know something? What?*
Quem vai comigo?	*Who is coming with me?*
Quanto é, por favor?	*How much is it, please?*
Quais queres?	*Which ones do you want?*
Há **quantas** pessoas?	*How many people are there?*

Adverbs

Como...?	*How? (in what way / what like)*
Quando...?	*When?*
Onde...?	*Where?*
Porque...? [BP = Por que...?]	*Why...?*
Porquê? [BP = Por quê?]	*Why? (when it stands alone)*

Como se diz ... em inglês?	*How do you say ... in English?*
Quando vamos sair?	*When are we going out?*
Onde está o meu livro?	*Where is my book?*
Porque não quer ir?	*Why don't you want to go?*

Interrogatives with prepositions

Some of these interrogatives may also be used in conjunction with certain prepositions. Here are some of the more common combinations:

Para quem?	*For whom?*
Com quem?	*With whom?*
De quem?	*Of whom, whose?*
Aonde?	*Where to?*
Para onde?	*Where to?*
De onde, donde?	*From where?*
Em que?	*In which?*

Com quem vai à festa?	*With whom are you going to the party?*
Para onde vão nas férias?	*Where are you going in the holidays?*

Em que rua deixámos [BP = deixamos] o carro? — *In which street did we leave the car?*

Portuguese questions often use **é que** in an extended interrogative form (like the French *est-ce que*) to add emphasis.

Onde é que nós vamos? — *Where is it that we're going?*
Porque é que o comboio [BP = trem] parou? — *Why is it that the train has stopped?*

Exclamations

Que…!	*What…, what a…, how…!*
Como!	*What / How…!*
Quanto / a…!	*How much…!*
Quantos / as…!	*How many…! / What a lot…!*
Qual / quais…!	*What, indeed / How great…!*
Quem…!	*If only…!*

Que sorte!	*What luck!*
Que azar!	*What bad luck!*
Como! É capaz de fazer isto?	*What! So you're capable of doing this?*

Quantas pessoas, meu Deus!	*Goodness me, what a lot of people!*

Qual prémio!	*Prize indeed!*
Quem me dera ter muito dinheiro!	*If only I had a lot of money!*

Don't forget that the intonation of your voice is vital to adding colour to exclamations. Learn how to do this properly by listening to how people use these expressions in the Portuguese-speaking world.

Exercises

A Decide on an appropriate interrogative to start each of these questions. The answer to each one should give you a clue.

1 ..QUEM.. escreveu Macbeth? — Shakespeare.
2 ..ONDE.. é o Rio de Janeiro? — No Brasil.
3 ..QUANDO.. é que o Brasil foi descoberto? — Em 1500.
4 ..COMO.. anos tens? — 36 anos.
5 ..COMO.. está? — Estou bem.
6 ..QUANTAS.. horas há num dia? — 24 horas.
7 ..PORQUE.. não foi à festa? — Estava doente.
8 ..ONDE.. faz anos? — No dia 15 de Setembro.
9 .... é o seu novo carro? — É grande e verde.
10 ..QUEM.. é o teu jogador de futebol preferido? — Luís Figo.

B Change the underlined words to negatives, to alter these sentences from affirmative statements to negative ones. You may need to add to, or re-arrange parts of them.

1 <u>Sempre</u> vamos de férias em Junho [BP = junho].
2 <u>Alguém</u> está na casa.
3 <u>Sempre</u> gosto de viajar com amigas.
4 Nós comemos <u>tudo</u>.
5 Gostas de leite? <u>Sim</u>, gosto.
6 Há lojas em <u>todas as partes</u> da cidade.
7 Tenho <u>alguma</u> informação importante.
8 Gostam <u>do</u> filme e·<u>da</u> música.
9 Ele sabe <u>tudo</u> sobre isto.
10 <u>Alguém</u> chegou hoje.

Grammar in context

The following three verses from different sonnets written by the Portuguese poet Florbela Espanca illustrate negatives, interrogatives and exclamations. Can you find examples in each verse?

1 Nesse triste convento aonde eu moro
  Noites e dias rezo e grito e choro
  E ninguém ouve... ninguém vê... ninguém...

[From: *A minha Dor*]

2 Chuva... tenho tristeza! Mas porquê?
  Vento... tenho saudades! Mas de quê?
  Ó neve que destino triste o nosso!

[From: *Neurastenia*]

3 E os meus vinte e três anos... (sou tão nova!)
  Dizem baixinho a rir: «Que linda a vida!...»
  Responde a minha Dor: «Que linda a cova!»

[From: *Dizeres íntimos*]

Verse	Negatives	Interrogatives	Exclamations
1			
2			
3			

12

prefixes and suffixes

In this unit you will learn
- how prefixes and suffixes alter the meaning of a word
- how to express affection, awe or criticism by using diminutives and augmentatives

Grammar in focus

Prefixes

Prefixes are small elements added on to the beginning of a word which change its basic meaning. Knowing *how* a prefix can alter a word a) helps you guess an unknown word in context and b) encourages you to learn related words, so that you more quickly build up a broader vocabulary base. The most common prefixes in Portuguese are as follows (and if you have studied Latin you will recognize many of them):

- **a- / an-** = not having something / lacking

  anormal *abnormal*   analfabetismo *illiteracy*

- **co- / com- / con-** = joining / with

  coexistir *to co-exist*   compartilhar *to share*
  concordar *to agree*

- **de- / des-** = opposite / contrary action

  decrescente *decreasing*   desfazer *to undo*

- **e- / em- / en-** and **i- / im- / in-** = inwards movement

  encarar *to face*   imigrar *to immigrate*
  importar *to import*

- **e- / em- / en-** *also* = a change of state involved

  evaporar *to evaporate*   embebedar *to get drunk*
  engordar *to get fat*

- **e- / ex-** = movement away

  emigrar *to emigrate*
  expelir *to expel*

- **i- / im- / in- / ir-** = negative

  ilegítimo *illegitimate*   imperfeito *imperfect*
  infeliz *unhappy*   irresponsável *irresponsible*

- **per-** = movement through or by

  percurso *route, journey*   perdurar *to last a long time*
  perene *everlasting, perennial*

- **pre-** = prior, previous

  previsão do tempo   precaução *precaution*
     weather forecast   preceder *to precede*

- **re-** = repetition, movement in opposite direction

  reabertura *re-opening* reagir *to react*
  reciclar *to recycle*

Suffixes

Suffixes are small additions to the end of words that give those words additional meaning. They can indicate larger or smaller size, change adjectives and verbs into nouns, and transform one noun into others. The commonest suffixes are **-mente** (for adverbs), **-inho**, **-zinho**, **-zito**, **-ão**, **-zarrão**, **-ona**, **-zada** and **-zeiro**.

General formation

If a word ends in a consonant, the suffix is added to the full word form, unless the word ends in **-m**, **-ão** or **-l** and is used with a suffix beginning with **z**. In this case, **-m** becomes **-n**. Plural forms drop the final **-s** before the suffix.

a manhã *morning* a manhãzinha *early morning*
os pães *loaves of bread* os pãezinhos *rolls*

Diminutives

Diminutives (**-(z)inho**, **-(z)ito**, **-isco**, **-ino**) are used to describe a person or object as small or cute, and can denote affection.

Words ending in unstressed **-o** or **-a** lose that ending and add on **-inho** or **-inha**. Other words usually add **-zinho** or **-zinha**. Some others you will pick up as you go along.

a mesa	*table*	a mesinha	*little table*
pobre	*poor*	pobrezinho	*poor little thing*
a mãe	*mother*	a mãezinha	*dear mother, mum(my)*
o José	*José*	o Zé / Zezinho	*little José (Joe / Joey)*
o gato	*cat*	o gatinho	*kitten*
um pouco	*a little*	um pouquinho	*a tiny little bit*
a filha	*daughter*	a filhinha	*young / little girl, dear daughter*
o rapaz	*lad, boy*	o rapazinho	*little lad*
pequeno	*small*	pequenino	*tiny*
a chuva	*rain*	o chuvisco	*drizzle*

Augmentatives

Augmentatives (**-ão**, **-zarrão**, **-ona**, **-oso**) are used to describe a person or object as large, strong or ugly, and can be pejorative. In the case of **-ão**, it is added onto words ending in a consonant, and replaces the final letter of most words ending in vowels. Feminine nouns become masculine in the -ão augmentative. -zarrão follows the rules for suffixes beginning with -z. -ona is used for words describing girls and women.

a carta	*letter*	o cartão	*card, cardboard*
a garrafa	*bottle*	o garrafão	*demi-john, carafe*
a solteira	*single woman*	a solteirona	*spinster*
a porta	*door*	o portão	*gate*
a sala	*room*	o salão	*large room*
o gato	*cat*	o gatão	*big cat*
a chuva	*rain*	chuvoso	*raining heavily*
a pimenta	*pepper* (condiment)	um pimentão	*pepper* (vegetable)
a palavra	*word*	um palavrão	*swear word*

Both diminutive and augmentative forms can be awkward to use correctly and require practice at first. Diminutive forms are extremely common in Portuguese.

Other common suffixes

-ada or -ado denote -*ful*, a group of / an abundance of.

o papel	*paper*	a papelada	*paperwork / piles of paper*
a colher	*spoon*	a colherada	*spoonful*
o punho	*fist*	o punhado	*handful*
o ninho	*nest*	a ninhada	*brood*
a noite	*night*	a noitada	*long night (out)*

-ria or -aria indicate the place where an article is made or sold.

a fruta	*fruit*	a frutaria	*fruit shop*
o tabaco	*tobacco*	a tabacaria	*tobacconist's*
o pão	*bread*	a padaria	*bakery / bread shop*
o papel	*paper*	a papelaria	*stationer's*
o sapato	*shoe*	a sapataria	*shoe shop*
o leite	*milk*	a leitaria	*dairy*

-eira or -eiro indicate the tree a fruit or plant has come from.

a maçã	*apple*	a macieira	*apple tree*
a amêndoa	*almond*	a amendoeira	*almond tree*
o limão	*lemon*	o limoeiro	*lemon tree*
o figo	*fig*	a figueira	*fig tree*
a rosa	*rose*	a roseira	*rose bush*

-ez / a, -ura, -dade, -ância, -ência and -dão change adjectives into nouns, usually abstract ones.

belo	*beautiful*	beleza	*beauty*
branco	*white*	brancura	*whiteness*
feliz	*happy*	felicidade	*happiness*
elegante	*elegant*	elegância	*elegance*
violento	*violent*	violência	*violence*
lento	*slow*	lentidão	*slowness*

-dor / a change a verb into the person performing the action when added to the infinitive of a verb, after dropping the final -r.

vender	*to sell*	vendedor / vendedora	*sales person*
navegar	*to navigate*	navegador / a	*sailor / navigator*
trabalhar	*to work*	trabalhador / a	*worker*
desenhar	*to design*	desenhador / a	*designer*
pescar	*to fish*	pescador / a	*fisherman / woman*
cobrar	*to charge*	cobrador / a	*money collector / (bus) conductor*

There are many other suffixes to look out for. When you start to spot patterns of endings, try to note the words into pattern groups. A few more to get you started are: **-al / -ano / -ção / -gem / -ismo / -vel**.

Exercises

A Solve the clues and find the words on the wordsearch grid.

1 A small table ~~MESINHA~~
2 You would get a lot of wine in this. ~~GARAFA~~
3 Overworked teachers have too much of this. ~~PAPELADA~~
4 where you would buy **sapatos** ~~SAPATARIA~~
5 from where you would pluck a fig ~~FIGUEIRO~~
6 Red tape works at this speed. ~~LENTO~~
7 a travelling .... ~~VENDEDOR~~
8 a cat to be reckoned with (also the name of a Portuguese **Vinho Verde**) ~~GATÃO~~
9 can you guess where you might buy **um livro** (*a book*)? ~~LIVRARIA~~
10 If something is **belo**, it has .... ~~BELEZA~~ ~~PAPELARIA~~

G	A	I	R	A	T	A	P	A	S
A	Z	A	B	C	Õ	E	F	A	H
R	E	K	L	M	A	V	P	I	A
R	L	U	V	W	D	E	Z	R	D
A	E	M	E	S	I	N	H	A	A
F	B	N	O	P	T	D	S	R	L
Ã	W	X	Y	Z	N	E	C	V	E
O	Ã	T	A	G	E	D	M	I	P
P	Q	R	S	T	L	O	W	L	A
F	I	G	U	E	I	R	A	H	P

B Match up the words on the left with any from the box on the right. Some may have more than one linked word.

1 casa
2 feliz
3 contente
4 cartinha
5 ver
6 moral
7 gato
8 pôr
9 fazer
10 imperfeito

> casinha   refazer
> perfazer   prever   infeliz
> perfeito   rever
> felizmente   gatinho   compor
> carta   casarão   descontente
> descompor   cartão
> gatão   desfazer
> amoral

Grammar in context

1 What does the name of the restaurant mean? What is the original word it came from?

Restaurante

PORTINHO

Rua dos Pescadores - Tel. 911 577 - 4910 VILA PRAIA DE ANGORA

Especialidades:

Peixes Frescos

Caldeirada de Congro

Caldeirada de Ruivo

Arroz de Tamboril

Parrilhada de Peixe

Taco na Pedra

Bife Pimenta

2 Which two diminutive forms are used to describe how your children will change on Saturdays?

☼ **PASSEIOS DE VERÃO – Parque dos Olivais**

Programação Infanto–Juvenil

Dia 15 Leituras com música
Dia 22 Circo Russo

Todos os sábados, os seus diabinhos
viram-se anjinhos!

13

todo, ambos and cada

In this unit you will learn
- how to use **todo** to talk about all or the whole, **ambos** (*both*) and **cada** (*each / every*)

Grammar in focus

Todo

Todo / toda / todos / todas (*all*, *every*, *the whole*) agree in number and gender with any corresponding noun. They are usually accompanied by the definite article (o / a / os / as), although in Brazil this is commonly omitted.

todo o dia [BP = todo dia]	*the whole day* [NB In Brazil this is often the phrase used to mean *every day*]
Toda a casa está suja.	*The whole house is dirty.*
Todos os papéis estão na pasta.	*All the papers are in the folder.*
Todas as mesas estavam ocupadas.	*All the tables were taken.*

Translated as *all* or *the whole*, **todo** can be placed either before or after the noun.

todo o Verão / o Verão todo   *all summer, the whole summer*

The definite article (the word for *the*) can be omitted when the word accompanying **todo** does not normally call for an article.

Fomos nós todos.	*All of us went.*
Todas estas flores foram plantadas no ano passado.	*All these flowers were planted last year.*

Adverbial use

Todo / a can also be used in the singular as an adverb. It should agree with the noun / adjective.

Tem o braço todo sujo.	*Your arm is all dirty.*
A janela está toda partida.	*The window is completely broken.*

Tudo

Tudo (*all*, *everything*) is a neuter pronoun which never changes form. It is used to refer to non-specific things or situations.

Eu nunca me lembro de tudo.	*I never remember everything.*
Tudo isto é uma maravilha.	*All of this is fantastic.*
Depois de tudo, ela voltou ao Japão.	*After everything, she returned to Japan.*

Other useful expressions

em / por toda a parte	*everywhere*
toda a gente / todos	*everybody*
todo o homem que...	*every man who...*
vi-as todas	*I saw them* (f.) *all / all of them*
primeiro que tudo	*first of all*
ao todo	*in all / altogether*
todo o possível	*everything possible*

Ambos

Ambos / as (*both*), like **todo**, can be used with a definite article when describing a noun, or without when used with pronouns or demonstratives.

Ambos os amigos jogam golfe.	*Both friends play golf.*
Ambas aquelas saias são bonitas.	*Both those skirts are pretty.*
Ambos partiram.	*They both left.*
Nós ambos fomos ao teatro.	*We both went to the theatre.*

You can also translate *both* by **os dois / as duas** (*the two*).

Os dois foram ao cinema.	*The two of them (both) went to the cinema.*

Cada

Cada (*each, every*) does not vary in form. It is used without a definite article and serves for both singular and plural nouns.

Há um autocarro [BP = ônibus] cada 30 minutos.	*There is a bus every 30 minutes.*
Tome o remédio cada três horas.	*Take the medicine every three hours.*
Cada um deles ganhou um prémio.	*Each one of them won a prize.*

Exercises

A Complete the following table with the correct forms of **todo**, **ambos** and **cada**. You may need to add the definite articles where required.

Masc. singular	Fem. singular	Masc. plural	Fem. plural
todo o inverno .... este mês (*month*)	.... loja a Primavera (*Spring*) .... a perna está .... torcida (*twisted*)	.... alunos todos aqueles dias	.... as pessoas fomos nós ....
		ambos os irmãos .... partiram	.... casas .... aquelas
cada dia	.... uma é bonita	.... 40 minutos	.... cinco semanas

B Can you translate the following? Help with vocabulary is given below.

1 O chapéu está todo sujo.
2 Toda a gente queria ir ao teatro.
3 Passamos o Verão todo na praia.
4 Quero comprar tudo.
5 Há um barco cada três (3) dias.
6 São 6,75 euros ao todo.
7 Vou fazer todo o possível para melhorar.
8 Todos os museus estão fechados hoje.
9 Ambas estas casas são bonitas.
10 Toda pessoa tem um bilhete.

o chapéu	*hat*	**vou fazer**	*I'm going to do*
sujo	*dirty*	**melhorar**	*to improve*
queria	*wanted*	**fechados**	*closed*
passamos	*we spend*	**hoje**	*today*
na praia	*on the beach*	**tem**	*has*
quero	*I want*	**um bilhete**	*a ticket*
comprar	*to buy*	**barco**	*boat*
são	*that's (lit. they are)*		

C Look at this letter from someone looking for a correspondent, and see if you can work out the following:

1 how often he plays football
2 what kind of music he likes
3 how many of his sisters work in the hospital
4 what he does every day
5 why he likes everything in the Algarve

> ### Olá!
>
> Eu sou o João, tenho 22 anos, e vivo no Algarve. Todos os fins-de-semana jogo futebol, e passo o verão todo na praia. Gosto de todo tipo de música, de animais, e de desporto [BP = esporte]. Tenho duas irmãs, e ambas trabalham no hospital. As duas são enfermeiras. Eu sou vendedor de 'Timeshare' e todos os dias visito todas as partes do Algarve. Adoro tudo cá, é tudo muito bonito.
>
> Escrevam-me!
>
> *João*

Grammar in context

1 Who can buy all they need here?

**ALUGUER
DE
QUARTOS**

Auto Mercado MALANGE

Fábrico próprio de Confeitaria – Cafetaria
TUDO PARA AS DONAS DE CASA

Telefone, 255 213 373
R. Dr. Joaquim Cotta, 14-18   4560-506 Penafiel

2 a How often can you get the best Sushi buffet?
   b Is it pre-prepared food?

Todos os dias
temos o melhor
buffet de
SUShi
a kilo
tudo feito na hora.

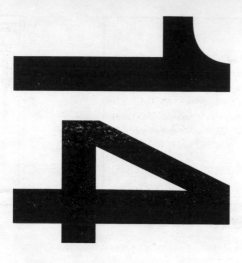

14

numerals

In this unit you will learn
- cardinal numbers (one to one million): how to say and write them in Portuguese
- ordinal numbers (first, second, etc.) and their use in Portuguese

Grammar in focus

Cardinal numbers

0	zero	30	trinta
1	um, uma	31	trinta e um / uma
2	dois, duas	32	trinta e dois / duas
3	três	40	quarenta
4	quatro	50	cinquenta
			[BP = cinqüenta]
5	cinco	60	sessenta
6	seis	70	setenta
7	sete	80	oitenta
8	oito	90	noventa
9	nove	100	cem, cento
10	dez	101	cento e um / uma
11	onze	110	cento e dez
12	doze	200	duzentos (as)
13	treze	300	trezentos (as)
14	catorze*	400	quatrocentos (as)
15	quinze	500	quinhentos (as)
16	dezasseis	600	seiscentos (as)
	[BP = dezesseis]		
17	dezassete	700	setecentos (as)
	[BP = dezessete]		
18	dezoito	800	oitocentos (as)
19	dezanove	900	novecentos (as)
	[BP = dezenove]		
20	vinte	1.000	mil
21	vinte e um / uma	2.000	dois mil
22	vinte e dois / duas	100.000	cem mil
23	vinte e três	1.000.000	um milhão
24	vinte e quatro	2.000.000	dois milhões
25	vinte e cinco	1.000.000.000	mil milhões

In Brazil, **um bilhão** is equivalent to one billion (1 followed by nine zeros).

*In Brazil you will often find the alternative **quatorze**.

Numbers *one* and *two* have both masculine and feminine forms.

quarenta e duas mesas	*42 tables*
cento e uma casas	*101 houses*

Numbers in the hundreds also have two forms:

duzentas caravanas	*200 caravans*
oitocentas e trinta e duas cervejas	*832 beers*

Above one thousand, numbers are always expressed in thousands and hundreds, and not as multiples of a hundred (as in the English *twelve hundred and fifty*), hence the year 1752 is **mil, setecentos e cinquenta e dois**.

The word **e** (*and*) appears between hundreds, tens and single digits: **cento e oitenta e dois** (*182*)

E appears after thousands in the following circumstances only:

- when the thousand is followed directly by a numeral from 1 to 100
- when the thousand is followed by a numeral from 200 to 900, if the last two numbers are zeros

quatro mil e sessenta e cinco	*4,065*
oito mil e quinhentos	*8,500*
mil novecentos e noventa e cinco	*1,995*
três mil quatrocentos e trinta	*3,430*

In Portuguese, a full stop is inserted after thousands etc., instead of a comma. Hence 1,532 is written 1.532, and 252,000 is 252.000.

A is not translated before **cem**, **cento** or **mil**.

Cem libras	*(a) hundred pounds*
Mil dólares	*(a) thousand dollars*

Cem is used for a round 100, **cento** for 101+.

Ordinal numbers

1st	primeiro(-a, -os, -as)	17th	décimo sétimo
2nd	segundo	18th	décimo oitavo
3rd	terceiro	19th	décimo nono
4th	quarto	20th	vigésimo
5th	quinto	21st	vigésimo primeiro
6th	sexto	22nd	vigésimo segundo
7th	sétimo	30th	trigésimo
8th	oitavo	40th	quadragésimo
9th	nono	50th	quinquagésimo [BP = qüinquagésimo]
10th	décimo	60th	sexagésimo
11th	décimo primeiro	70th	septuagésimo [BP = setuagésimo]
12th	décimo segundo	80th	octagésimo
13th	décimo terceiro	90th	nonagésimo
14th	décimo quarto	100th	centésimo
15th	décimo quinto	1000th	milésimo
16th	décimo sexto		

Ordinals may be abbreviated by using the appropriate number, plus the last vowel of the number (**o** or **a**). This is clearly seen in addresses:

Moro no 12° (décimo segundo) *I live on the twelfth floor.*
  andar.

Ordinals agree in number and gender with the noun to which they refer. In the compound versions (**décimo primeiro, décimo segundo, vigésimo primeiro,** etc.), both parts of the number agree.

a décima quinta janela   *the fifteenth window*

Ordinals are not used very frequently in Portuguese beyond tenth, except in addresses, particularly for the number of the floor in apartment blocks. In reference to popes, royalty, and centuries, ordinals are used up to tenth, and from there on cardinal numbers are introduced. In both cases, the numbers follow the titles.

João Primeiro	*John the First*
o século quinto	*the fifth century*
Manuel Doze	*Manuel the Twelfth*
o século vinte e um	*the twenty-first century*

Exercises

A Write out, or say, these numbers in full.

1	14	5	199	9	3.600
2	36	6	450	10	26.842
3	78	7	1.065	11	246.000
4	121	8	1.344	12	1.532.912

B Decide whether these numbers are written correctly or not. If they are not, correct what is wrong.

58	cinquenta e oito	122	cento e sessenta e cinco
134	cem e trinta e quatro	1.018	dois mil, zero e oito
25	vinte cinco	4.222	seis mil, dois dois dois
521	quatrocentos e trinta e um	10.653	dez mil, seiscentos e cinquenta e três
46	quarenta e seis	912	nove cem doze

C Choose the correct ordinals to fill the gaps.

		a	b	c
1	Pedro (I)	um	primeiro	décimo
2	Moramos no (16) .... andar	décimo sexto	dezasseis	décimo sétimo
3	O século (VIII)	oito	ochenta	oitavo
4	A (22) .... casa	vigésimo segundo	vigésima segunda	vigésimo segunda
5	Luís (XIV)	catorze	décimo quarto	quinze
6	É o (80th) .... aniversário	oitenta	dezoito	octagésimo

Grammar in context

The euro in Portugal is known as **o euro,** divided into 100 **cêntimos.** A price such as € 7,60 may be rendered **sete (euros) e sessenta (cêntimos),** although until the new currency really beds down, it is likely that variations on how it is conveyed will be widespread.

Look at this price list for magazine subscriptions and answer the questions, writing out prices in full if required.

Revistas	No. de edições	Desconto	Europa			Resto do mundo		
			Assinatura c/desconto (€)	Despesas de envio (€)	Total a pagar (€)	Assinatura c/desconto (€)	Despesas de envio (€)	Total a pagar (€)
Exame	25	26%	44,40	46,60	91	44,40	100,60	145
Executive Digest	12	20%	27,80	25,20	53	27,80	51,20	79
Exame Informática	12	20%	25,90	25,35	51,25	25,90	51,35	77,25
Visão	26	30%	39,90	32,55	72,45	39,90	58,50	98,40
Casa Claudia	15	20%	39	52	91	39	106	145
Super Interessante	12	16%	19,50	25,50	45	19,50	51,50	71
Turbo	12	20%	26,85	41,25	68,10	26,85	89,15	116
Cosmopolitan	12	15%	22,95	41,55	64,50	22,95	84,90	107,85
Disney especial	12	42%	17,25	17,75	35	17,25	26,75	44
Barbie	12	20%	18,20	15	33,20	18,20	27	45,20

1 How much is the total cost of a subscription to *Exame* if you live in Europe? Write it out in full.
2 How many issues (**edições**) of *Visão* do you get? (Write out the number.)
3 What discount is there (= **por cento**) on *Turbo*?
4 If you live outside Europe, what's the cost of the discount subscription to *Barbie*?
5 How much are the mailing costs in Europe for *Exame Informática*?
6 Which magazine offers a discount of **dezasseis por cento**?

15

measures and dimensions

In this unit you will learn
- how to express arithmetic, fractions and decimals in Portuguese
- ways of talking about dimensions and units of measure
- points of the compass

Grammar in focus

Arithmetical signs

+ e / mais   adição   3 + 2 = 5 Três mais dois são cinco.
− menos   subtracção   9 − 6 = 3 Nove menos seis dão três.
x vezes /   multiplicação   2 x 2 = 4 Dois vezes dois são
  multiplicado por   quatro.
÷ dividido por   divisão   10 ÷ 2 = 5 Dez dividido por dois
                                dá cinco.

= são, dá, dão, é igual a

somar *to add*   multiplicar *to multiply*   subtrair *to subtract*
dividir *to divide*   calcular   *to calculate*   o algarismo *sum*

Fractions

½	um meio	⅙	um sexto
⅓	um terço	⅐	um sétimo
¼	um quarto	⅛	um oitavo
¾	três quartos	⅑	um nono
⅕	um quinto	$\frac{1}{10}$	um décimo

Decimals

In Portuguese, the decimal point is represented by a comma, and
not a full stop. Hence, 4.8 is written as 4,8 and 0.001 is 0,001.
The comma is subsequently part of the decimal as it is written
or spoken in full.

4,8 = quatro **vírgula** oito

0,001 = zero **vírgula** zero zero um

Dimensions

Ter (*to have*), **ser** (*to be*), **medir** (*to measure*) and **pesar** (*to weigh*) are verbs used in measurements.

Nouns		Adjectives	
a altura / a elevação	*height*	alto	*high, tall*
o comprimento	*length*	comprido	*long*
a largura	*width*	largo	*wide*
a profundidade	*depth*	profundo	*deep*
a grossura	*thickness*	grosso	*thick*
o peso	*weight*	pesado	*heavy*

A sala tem três metros de **comprimento** e dois de **largura**.	*The room is three metres long by two metres wide.*
O mar tem duas braças de **profundidade**.	*The sea is two fathoms deep.*
A casa mede sete metros de **elevação**.	*The house is seven metres tall.*

Units of measure, metric system

quilómetro*	hectómetro	decâmetro	metro	decímetro	centímetro	milímetro
km	hm	dam	m	dm	cm	mm

quilograma	hectograma	decagrama	grama	decigrama	centigrama	miligrama
kg	hg	dag	g	dg	cg	mg

quilolitro	hectolitro	decalitro	litro	decilitro	centilitro	mililitro
kl	hl	dal	l	dl	cl	ml

*[BP = quilômetro]

Area / Volume

$1m^2$ = um metro quadrado $4m^2$ = quatro metros quadrados
$1m^3$ = um metro cúbico $5m^3$ = cinco metros cúbicos

Other units of measure

a polegada	*inch*	o quartilho	*pint*
o pé	*foot*	o galão	*gallon*
a jarda	*yard*	a libra	*pound*
a milha	*mile*	a tonelada	*ton*

Geometrical terms

Plane surfaces

a linha	*line*	o rectângulo	*rectangle*
o ângulo	*angle*	o rombóide	*rhomboid*
o ângulo recto	*right angle*	o círculo	*circle*
[BP = reto]		o ângulo agudo	*acute angle*
o ângulo obtuso	*obtuse angle*	o diâmetro	*diameter*
o triângulo	*triangle*	o raio	*radius*
o quadrado	*square*	o polígano	*polygon*
o perímetro	*perimeter*		

Solids

o cubo	*cube*	a pirâmide	*pyramid*
o cilindro	*cylinder*	o cone	*cone*
a esfera	*sphere*	o prisma	*prism*
o hemisfério	*hemisphere*		

Other measurement language

uma régua	*ruler*	o valor	*value*
o dobro	*double*	a medida	*measurement*
a metade	*half*	maior	*greater / bigger*
a velocidade	*speed*	menor	*lesser / smaller*
a amplitude	*space / extent*	a área	*area*
o recipiente	*container*	a quantidade	*quantity*

The points of the compass

o norte
north

o noroeste *north-west*   *north-east* o nordeste

o oeste   o leste (este)
west   *east*

o sudoeste *south-west*   *south-east* o sudeste

south
o sul

Exercises

A Write out these numerical expressions in full in Portuguese.

1 125 + 75 = 200
2 85 – 35 = 50
3 16 x 4 = 64
4 1000 ÷ 10 = 100
5 ⅖

6 ³/₁₀
7 ⅝
8 17,2
9 2,56
10 13 m²

B Look at the design for a new apartment and complete the table with the relevant measurements in figures.

	Comprimento	Largura	Área	Perímetro
Quarto 1				
Quarto 2				
Cozinha				
Apartamento – total				

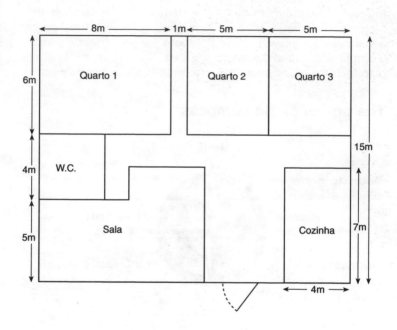

Language watch 3

Most words in Portuguese ending in **-dade** correspond to the English ending *-ity*:

cidade *city*   caridade *charity*   electricidade *electricity*
felicidade *felicity (= happiness)*   capacidade *capacity*
luminosidade *luminosity (light)*   qualidade *quality*
claridade *clarity*   nacionalidade *nationality*

They are all feminine nouns in Portuguese.

16

time

In this unit you will learn
- days of the week, months and seasons of the year
- how to express dates and times in Portuguese
- some other useful time expressions

Grammar in focus

Days of the week – *os dias da semana*

(a) segunda-feira	*Monday*
(a) terça-feira	*Tuesday*
(a) quarta-feira	*Wednesday*
(a) quinta-feira	*Thursday*
(a) sexta-feira	*Friday*
(o) sábado	*Saturday*
(o) domingo	*Sunday*

Weekdays are feminine, and it is common in the spoken language to drop the -feira suffix from each one. The days of the weekend are masculine. There appears to be little consensus as to whether they are written with a capital letter or not.

The prepositions **em** and **a** are used with days of the week.

na sexta-feira	*on Friday*
nas terças	*on Tuesdays*
O barco parte **às** quartas e **às** sextas.	*The boat departs on Wednesdays and Fridays.*
Amanhã é domingo.	*Tomorrow is Sunday.*
Vamos visitar os amigos **na segunda.**	*We're going to visit friends on Monday.*
Todos **os domingos** eles vão à missa.	*They go to Mass every Sunday*
Quinta de manhã, vamos à piscina.	*On Thursday morning we're going to the swimming pool.*

Months of the year – *os meses do ano*

Janeiro	*January*	Julho	*July*
Fevereiro	*February*	Agosto	*August*
Março	*March*	Setembro	*September*
Abril	*April*	Outubro	*October*
Maio	*May*	Novembro	*November*
Junho	*June*	Dezembro	*December*

Seasons of the year – *as estações do ano*

a Primavera	*spring*	o Outono	*autumn*
o Verão	*summer*	o Inverno	*winter*

In Brazil, capital letters are generally not used for months or seasons.

Special holidays – *férias / feriados* (bank or national holidays)

a Passagem do Ano / o Reveillon	*New Year's Eve*
o Ano Novo	*New Year*
o Carnaval	*Carnival*
a Quaresma	*Lent*
a Páscoa	*Easter*
o Natal	*Christmas*

Dates

Cardinal numbers (*one*, *two*, *three*, etc.) are used with dates, including the first – (**o dia**) **um**. However, the 1st January is usually still referred to as **o Primeiro de Janeiro** = New Year's Day.

Que data é hoje?	*What date is it today?*
Quantos são hoje?	*What is the date today?*
A quantos estamos?	*What's the date?* [lit. *At what (day) are we?*]
É o dia vinte e três.	*It's the twenty-third.*
Hoje são onze.	*It's the eleventh today.*
Estamos a vinte e dois.	*It's the twenty-second.*
Estávamos a / no dia 15 de Maio.	*It was the 15th May.*
É o quinze de Setembro.	*It's the 15th of September.*
Nasceu a seis de Julho de 1971.	*He was born on 6th July 1971.*
Casaram-se no dia 11 de Agosto.	*They got married on 11th August.*
Era (o dia) 25 de Novembro.	*It was the 25th November.*
Era o Primeiro de Janeiro.	*It was New Year's Day (1st January).*
A festa será no dia 15 de Abril.	*The party will be on the 15th April.*

Divisions of time

o segundo	*second*	o dia	*day*
o minuto	*minute*	o mcio-dia	*mid-day*
a hora	*hour*	a meia-noite	*mid-night*
um quarto de hora	*¼ hour*	a semana	*week*
(uma) meia hora	*½ hour*	quinze dias	*fortnight*
a manhã	*morning*	o mês	*month*
a tarde	*afternoon*	o ano	*year*
a tarde / noite	*evening*	o século	*century*
a noite	*night*	o milénio	*millennium*

Expressions of time

agora	*now*	ontem	*yesterday*
agora mesmo	*right now*	anteontem	*the day before*
já	*right now /*		*yesterday*
	already	a semana passada	*last week*
hoje	*today*	a semana que vem	*next week*
esta manhã	*this morning*	/ a semana próxima	
esta noite	*tonight*		
esta tarde	*this afternoon* (said during the afternoon)		
logo à tarde	*this afternoon* (said during the morning)		
ontem à noite	*last night*	o mês passado	*last month*
anteontem à	*the night*	a quinta passada	*last Thursday*
noite	*before last*	o domingo que	*next Sunday*
amanhã	*tomorrow*	vem	
depois de	*the day after*	todo o dia / o dia	*all day*
amanhã	*tomorrow*	todo	
de / da	*early in the*	ao anoitecer	*at nightfall*
madrugada	*morning*	todos os dias	*every day*
de / da manhã	*in the*	[BP = todo dia] /	
	morning	cada dia	
de / da tarde	*in the*	todo (o) tempo	*all the time*
	afternoon /	ontem à tarde	*yesterday*
	evening		*afternoon*
à / da noite	*at night*	daqui a (uma	*in a (week's)*
amanhã de	*tomorrow*	semana)	*time*
manhã	*morning*		
ao amanhecer	*at daybreak*		
ao meio da semana		*in the middle of the week*	
ao / no princípio do mês		*at the beginning of the month*	
ao / no fim do ano		*at the end of the year*	
há (dois anos)		*(two years) ago*	

Time of day

Que horas são?	*What time is it?*
Que horas eram?	*What time was it?*
Tem as horas?	*Do you have the time?*
É a uma (hora).	*It's one o'clock.*
É meio-dia.	*It's midday.*
Era meia-noite.	*It was midnight.*
São duas (horas) da tarde.	*It's two in the afternoon.*

Time past the hour is denoted by adding the number of minutes, up to thirty, on to the hour, using the word **e** (*and*). If it is midday, midnight, or any time connected to one o'clock, you start the sentence with **é** (*it is*). For hours beyond that (two onwards), use **são** (*they are*), because you are dealing with hours in the plural.

São quatro **e dez**.	*It's ten past four.*
É uma **e um quarto**.	*It's a quarter past one.*

Time up to the hour can be expressed in three ways:

1 by subtracting the minutes from the nearest next full hour, using **menos**
2 by using the number of minutes to the hour + **para**
3 with **faltar** (*to be lacking*) + the number of minutes to the hour + **para**

São dez **menos vinte**.	*It's twenty to ten.*
São **cinco para** as três.	*It's five to three.*
Faltam dez para meia-noite.	*It's ten minutes before midnight.*
É **um quarto para** a uma.	*It's a quarter to one.*

A que horas...? At what time...?

A que horas parte / chega o barco?	At *what time does the boat depart / arrive?*
A que horas abre / fecha o banco?	At *what time does the bank open / close?*
A que horas começa / termina o filme?	At *what time does the film start / finish?*

The time at which something happens is expressed as in the previous section, but you change the start of the phrase to say *at...*, rather than *It's...*:

à uma hora	*at one o'clock*
ao meio-dia / à meia-noite	*at mid-day / at mid-night*

And for hours beyond one:

às quatro (horas)	*at four (o'clock)*
às três e meia	*at 3..30*
às oito menos vinte	*at 7.40*
às dez para as seis	*at ten to six* (**faltar** is not used here)

The twenty-four hour clock, commonly used in timetables, is often more straightforward, as you simply deal with the numbers in the order they appear.

O comboio [BP = trem] parte às **vinte e duas e quarenta**. — *The train leaves at 22:40.*

O barco chega às **quinze e vinte e nove**. — *The boat arrives at 15:29.*

Time from... until...

For this you use the prepositions **de** and **a**.

da uma / do meio-dia / da meia-noite — *from one o'clock / from midday / from midnight*

das quatro (horas) — *from four (o'clock)*

à uma / ao meio-dia/ à meia-noite — *'til one / to mid-day / to midnight*

às sete — *to / 'til seven*

às nove e meia — *to / 'til 9.30*

You can also use the word **até** (*until*) in expressions such as the following:

das oito até às nove — *from eight until nine*

A partir de is also used, especially if there is a set starting time for things such as meals in hotels, or events:

Servimos o pequeno-almoço [BP = café da manhã] a partir das sete horas. — *We serve breakfast from seven (onwards).*

Exercises

A Solve the clues to find the names of days, months and seasons on the grid. If you get them all correct, the letters down the middle spell out a season.

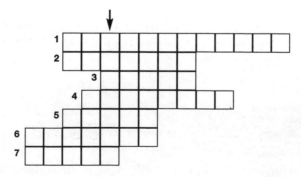

1 depois de quarta-feira
2 o primeiro mês do ano
3 uma estação quente
4 o mês antes de Outubro
5 Hoje é quarta, ontem era…
6 depois de sábado
7 o sétimo mês
The missing season is……………?

B Look at the calendar page below and see if you can work out the answers to the questions. The ringed date is the date today (**hoje**).

Abril de 200X

Seg.	Ter.	Qua.	Qui.	Sex.	Sáb.	Dom.
1	2	3	4	5	6	7
8	9	(10)	11	12	13 F	14
15 P	16	17	18	19	20	21
22	23	24	25 F	26	27	28
30						

1 A quantos estamos? …………
2 Há dois dias era o dia ………… .
3 Depois de amanhã será que dia da semana? …………
4 A terça que vem será o dia ………… .
5 Há feriados (F) nos dias ………… e ………… .
6 No dia quinze é ………… (*Easter*).
7 O dia um era uma ………… -feira.
8 O dia 27 será um ………… .

C Look at the times given for various things happening (travel, opening hours, meals), and answer the questions in Portuguese, writing the times out in full.

1 A que horas parte o comboio/trem?

08:00

2 A que horas está fechada a loja?

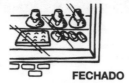

FECHADO

3 Que horas são?

4 Que horas eram
quando te vi
(*when I saw you*)?

5 A que horas chega o barco?

6 A que horas servem o pequeno-almoço / café da manhã?

Grammar in context

Read the opening times of the Museum in Oporto and see if you can work out:

1 what the normal opening hours on a Wednesday are
2 what time it closes on a Sunday during January
3 if you can visit it on a Monday in August.

Museu / Museum
3ª., 4ª. e 6ª. 10h00l19h00
5ª. 10h00l20h00
Sáb., Dom. e Feriados 10h00l20h00
(Abril a Setembro)
Sáb., Dom. e Feriados 10h00l19h00
(Outubro a Março)

7
personal pronouns

In this unit you will learn
- about subject pronouns in Portuguese (*I, you, he / she*, etc.)
- about direct object pronouns (*me, you, him / her*, etc.)
- about indirect object pronouns (*I gave the book to her*)
- about reflexive pronouns (*I wash myself*)
- where to position pronouns in the sentence
- how to combine pronouns where necessary

Grammar in focus

Subject pronouns

The subject of a verb is the person (or thing) carrying out the action, and can be represented by a pronoun in the first, second or third person, singular or plural, as follows:

	Singular		Plural	
1st	*I*	eu	*we*	nós
2nd	*you*	tu	*you*	vós
3rd	*he / it*	ele	*they* (m.)	eles
	she / it	ela	*they* (f.)	elas
	you	você	*you*	vocês

Forms of address (how you call someone *you*) can be complex, but in general, **tu**, the familiar form of *you*, is used with close friends, family, children, and pets. In many areas of Brazil, **você** – usually considered a more polite and formal second person singular form in Portugal – is used with almost everyone, and **tu** has a limited spread. Through the influence of Brazilian soap operas (**telenovelas**), the **você** form is heard more in Portugal now. The **vós** form is considered outdated, and is generally heard only in church services, public speeches, and amongst older speakers living in remote regions. **Vocês** is the accepted plural *you* form (apart from the alternative use of the very polite **os senhores / as senhoras**).

Note that Portuguese subject pronouns do not necessarily need to be used with the verb, as in many cases the verb ending denotes the subject. However, to avoid any ambiguity, pronouns should be used with the third person forms (which can mean *he*, *she*, *it*, *they* or *you*), unless there is no doubt as to who or what the subject is.

Object pronouns

Object pronouns receive the action of the verb. They can be direct, indirect or reflexive, and can be used with prepositions.

Direct object pronouns

The direct object directly receives the action of the verb. It responds to the direct questions *What...?* Or *Whom...?*

Singular		Plural	
me	*me*	nos	*us*
te	*you*	vos	*you*
o (m.)	*him; it; you*	os (m.)	*them; you*
a (f.)	*her; it; you*	as (f.)	*them; you*

Vejo-**os**.

I see them / you. (What / whom do I see?)

Ouviste-**nos**?

Did you hear us? (What / whom did you hear?)

Eles batem-**me**.

They beat me. (What / whom do they beat?)

In colloquial usage in Brazil, it is common practice for the pronouns **o / a / os / as** to be replaced by **ele / ela / eles / elas**.

Você viu eles?

Did you see them?

Changes to spelling following verbs

With direct object pronouns in the third person (**o, a, os, as**) certain changes occur in the following situations:

- Following verb forms ending in **-r, -s,** and **-z**.

  These final letters are omitted, and an **-l** is inserted before the pronoun. In the case of the omission of final **-r**, the following written accents are added to the remaining final vowel:

  -ar → -á
  -er → -ê
  -ir → -i (no accent)

  Accents are also required on compounds of the verb **pôr** (*to put*), e.g. **pô-lo**, and on **faz** (*make / do*), **traz** (*bring*), and **fez** (*did / made*). The verb form **quer** (*want*) takes on an extra **e**, in **quere-o** etc., and the two forms **tens** (*you have*) and **vens** (*you come*) become **tem-lo** and **vem-lo**, etc.

  Vou comprar a casa. Vou **comprá-la**.
  I'm going to buy the house. I'm going to buy it.

  Vendemos o carro. **Vendemo-lo**.
  We are selling the car. We are selling it.

  Quem fez os bolos? A Marta **fê-los**.
  Who made the cakes? Martha made them.

- Following verb forms ending in **-m, -ão** and **-õe** (nasal sounds). The endings are maintained, but an **n** is added before the pronoun to preserve the nasal sound.

Elas pintam a janela. Elas pintam-**na**.	*They paint the window. They paint it.*
Os alunos dão os livros ao professor. Os alunos dão-**nos** ao professor.	*The pupils give the books to the teacher. The pupils give them to the teacher.*
Põe o saco ali. Põe-**no** ali.	*Put the bag over there. Put it over there.*

All of these changes actually make it easier to pronounce the verb + pronoun forms, as they flow much better with these adaptations.

Indirect object pronouns

The indirect object has an indirect relation to the action of the verb. It denotes the person or thing *to* or *for whom* the action is performed. You can test out whether an indirect object pronoun is required by asking yourself if you can add the word *to* (or *for*) before the pronoun.

e.g. I gave the book to her.
I gave what? The book = direct object.
To whom? To her = indirect object.

Singular		Plural	
me	*to me*	nos	*to us*
te	*to you*	vos	*to you*
lhe	*to him, her, it, you*	lhes	*to them, you*

Deram-**nos** um bolo.	*They gave us a cake.*
Vendo-**lhe** o carro.	*I sell the car to her / him / you.*

Be careful, as in English we often omit the word *to* – *I sell her the car*. Go back to your basic questions of *What?* and *To whom?*

To avoid ambiguity with the indirect object pronoun in the third person, the following constructions can be used:

Vendo o carro **a ele** (etc.).	*I sell the car to him (etc.).*
Vendo a carro **à senhora** (etc.).	*I sell the car to you (very polite) (etc.).*

Reflexive pronouns

A reflexive pronoun accompanies an appropriate reflexive verb and refers back to the subject of that verb. Reflexive verbs are indicated in the dictionary by -**se**, attached to the infinitive. Some non-reflexive verbs can also be made reflexive. (See Unit 23 for more details.)

Singular	Plural
me *myself*	nos *ourselves*
te *yourself*	vos *yourselves*
se *himself, herself, itself, yourself*	se *themselves, yourselves*

Levanto-**me** às 8.   *I get up at 8 o'clock.*
Senta-**te** aqui.   *Sit here.*
Esqueceram-**se** da hora.   *They forgot the time.*

The final **-s** of the first person plural verb form is dropped before the reflexive.

Deitamos → Deitamo-nos cedo. *We go to bed early.*

Position of object pronouns

In Portugal, the object pronouns (direct, indirect, or reflexive), are usually attached to the end of the verb by a hyphen. However, in Brazil object pronouns are more often found preceding the verb in straightforward, affirmative sentences, especially when a subject pronoun is used.

Elas levantaram-**se** tarde.   *They got up late.*
[BP] Eu **me** chamo Edu.   *I'm called Edu.*

In both variants, the pronoun precedes the verb, without a hyphen, with the following:

- conjunctions (joining words)
- adverbs
- *that* clauses (**que** + verb: the word *that* is not always present in English)
- negative sentences
- interrogatives
- prepositions

One of my students noted that it may serve as a memory aid to keep in mind that the initials of this list spell out 'catnip'! If it works for you, try it!

Não quero ir porque me   *I don't want to go because I*
sinto mal.   *feel ill.*
Sempre te vejo na biblioteca.   *I always see you in the library.*
Queríamos que os vendessem.   *We would like you to sell them.*

Não lhe dei suficiente.   *I did not give her enough.*
Para quando o quer?   *For when do you want it?*

Position with the gerund

With the gerund (the *-ing* form of the verb – see Unit 31), the object pronoun follows and is joined by a hyphen, unless there is a negative, or the preposition **em**, or with **estar** and **ir**.

Vendo-a...	*(On) seeing her...*
Não o querendo ler...	*Not wanting to read it...*

Position with the infinitive

This is a slightly more complex matter, with many more permutations. There follows a brief overview; more elaborate constructions, particularly in the written language, can be added as you advance in your learning, and spot examples in reading:

- The (weak) object pronoun usually follows the infinitive, joined to it by a hyphen. However, when the infinitive follows a preposition, it is more common for the object pronoun to move in front of the infinitive, although it is often still found after it. The pronouns **o / a / os / as** do not contract and combine with the prepositions **de** and **em** on these occasions.

Querem comprá-los.	*They want to buy them*
Gostariam de nos visitar /	*They would like to visit us.*
Gostariam de visitar-nos.	

- With the preposition **a** (**ao**) and the infinitive, the pronoun goes after the infinitive.

Ao ver-te, não te reconheci.	*On seeing you, I didn't recognize you.*

- With the preposition **por**, if the direct object pronoun is in the third person (**o / a / os / as**), and is not combined with the indirect pronoun (see later sections), then it follows the infinitive.

Começou por dizê-lo a todos.	*He began by saying it to everyone.*

but

Acabou por mo dizer.	*He ended up telling (it to) me.*

- If the infinitive has been made negative, the pronoun goes before it.

para não te ofender	*in order not to offend you*

Position with the past participle

The pronouns do not combine with the past participle in any way. They are linked with the auxiliary verb (the verb used with the past participle – usually **ter**, **estar**, **ser** and others – see Units 31–3). Normal rules of position apply.

Tinha-a comprado.	*I had bought it.*
Não os tem visto ultimamente.	*He hasn't seen them recently.*

Position of pronouns with the future and conditional tenses

When a verb in either of the above tenses requires an object pronoun after it, the pronoun is inserted in the following fashion:

main verb part (infinitive) + pronoun + verb ending

Nós **falar-lhe-emos** amanhã.	*We will speak to him tomorrow.*

Normal rules of contraction apply:

Trá-**lo-iam** se estivessem cá.	*They would bring it if they were here.*

These forms are usually avoided in colloquial language, by omission of the object pronoun, or by the use of other tenses.

Falamos / Vamos falar com ele amanhã.
Trariam se estivessem cá.

Contracted object pronouns

When a sentence includes two object pronouns they join together, or form a contraction, with the indirect pronoun first, followed by the direct. The usual rules of position still apply.

Indirect + direct sing.	Indirect + direct plural
me + o → mo	nos + o → no-lo
me + a → ma	nos + a → no-la
me + os → mos	nos + os → no-los
me + as → mas	nos + as → no-las
te + o → to	vos + o → vo-lo
te + a → ta	vos + a → vo-la
te + os → tos	vos + os → vo-los
te + as → tas	vos + as → vo-las
lhe + o → lho	lhes + o → lho
lhe + a → lha	lhes + a → lha
lhe + os → lhos	lhes + os → lhos
lhe + as → lhas	lhes + as → lhas

Eles deram-mos.	*They gave them to me.*
Não vo-lo digo.	*I will not / cannot tell you.*
Mandou-ta?	*Did he send it to you?*
Deram-lhas.	*They gave them to them.*

Confusion may arise from the type of restricted construction found in this last example. To avoid this kind of ambiguity, use the prepositional forms **a ele, a ela, aos senhores,** etc.

| Deram-nas **aos senhores.** | *They gave them to you (polite).* |
| Deram-nas **a eles.** | *They gave them to them (masculine).* |

Brazilians tend to use this structure widely in everyday speech.

Deu-mos → Deu-os a mim → Deu-me

Avoidance of contracted forms

These awkward constructions are often spontaneously omitted from Portuguese, as too are the more simple object forms.

Dá-me 50 libras?	*Will you give me £50?*
Sim, dou.	*Yes, I will (give it to you).*
Gostou do filme?	*Did you like the film?*
Não, não gostei.	*No, I didn't (like it).*

Object pronouns with prepositions

When object pronouns follow a preposition, they take another form.

Singular		Plural	
mim	*me*	nós	*us*
ti	*you*	vós	*you*
ele	*him*	eles	*them*
ela	*her*	elas	*them*
si	*himself, herself, itself, yourself*	si	*themselves, yourselves*
você	*you, yourself*	vocês	*you, yourselves*

Ela esqueceu-se de mim.	*She forgot me.*
Não estou contra ti.	*I'm not against you.*
Fizeram o bolo para ela.	*They made the cake for her.*
Gosta de fazer coisas só para si.	*He likes to do things just for himself.*

To add clarity to a sentence, the appropriate forms of **mesmo /
a / os / as** or **próprio / a / os / as** may be added, both meaning
self / selves.

Ela trabalha para si **mesma**.	*She works for herself.*
Comprámos o bolo para nós **próprios**.	*We bought the cake for ourselves.*

Object pronouns with the preposition *com*

The object pronouns combine with the preposition **com** (*with*)
in the following ways:

Singular		Plural	
comigo	*with me*	connosco	*with us* [BP = conosco]
contigo	*with you*	convosco	*with you*
com ele	*with him*	com eles	*with them*
com ela	*with her*	com elas	*with them*
com você	*with you*	com vocês	*with you*
consigo	*with him(self), her(self), your(self)*	consigo	*with them(selves), your(selves)*

Quem vem comigo?	*Who's coming with me?*
Ele está a falar com elas.	*He's talking with them.*
Trouxeste o irmãozinho contigo?	*Have you brought your little brother with you?*

For a comprehensive view of prepositions, see Unit 9.

Overview of personal pronouns

Subject	Object				
	Direct	Indirect	Reflexive	+ Preposit. (except *com*)	+ com
eu	me	me	me	mim	comigo
tu	te	te	te	ti	contigo
ele	o	lhe	se	ele	com ele
ela	a	lhe	se	ela	com ela
você*	o / a	lhe	se	si / você	consigo / com você
nós	nos	nos	nos	nós	connosco [BP = conosco]
vós	vos	vos	vos	vós	convosco
eles	os	lhes	se	eles	com eles
elas	as	lhes	se	elas	com elas
vocês**	os / as (vos)	lhes (vos)	se	vocês	com vocês (convosco)

* Also for **o senhor / a senhora**
** Also for **os senhores / as senhoras**

Exercises

A Replace the underlined words with appropriate object pronouns, direct or indirect. Insert a hyphen where necessary, and alter any spelling or word order if you need to.

1 Vendo <u>os carros</u>.
2 Comprámos <u>a casa</u>.
3 Ele deu um livro <u>ao Pedro</u>.
4 Vou devolver (*to return*) <u>os sapatos</u> amanhã.
5 Viu (<u>*us*</u>) no parque.
6 Emprestas o carro <u>à Eduarda</u>?
7 Enviaram uma carta (<u>*to us*</u>).
8 Vê <u>o professor</u> todos os dias.
9 Visitamos (<u>tu</u>) esta semana.
10 Diz a verdade (*the truth*) (<u>*to them*</u>).

B Decide whether the pronouns are in the correct position and say 'yes' or 'no'. Make sure you understand why each one is where it is by checking back through the unit. Assume 'standard' European positionings throughout.

1 A porta abriu-se.
2 Já não me interessa.
3 Todas me admiram.
4 Porque é que nos chamou?
5 Não importa-se.
6 Estou contente por te ter encontrado.
7 Onde o encontraram?
8 Fique aqui enquanto lhe telefono.
9 Sempre vejo-o aos domingos.
10 Parece-nos muito interessante.

C Insert the correct pronouns in the spaces in the text about hiring a car. Choose from the box on the next page.

Miguel	Boa tarde, senhor Silva. Como está?
Sr Silva	Boa tarde, Miguel. Só um minutinho. Atendo- **(1)**............ já.
	(*A few minutes later...*)
Sr Silva	Então, em que **(2)**............ posso ser útil?
Miguel	Queria apresentar- **(3)**............ o meu colega John, que está a passar uns dias **(4)**............ . Precisa de alugar um carro.
Sr Silva	Claro. Quem vai usá- **(5)**............ ?
John	É só para **(6)**............ .
Sr Silva	Muito bem. Tem os documentos **(7)**............?
John	O Miguel tem- **(8)**............ aqui.
Sr Silva	Qual é o seu nome completo?

John	Chamo- **(9)**............	John Edward Church.
Sr Silva	Bom. O carro estará pronto mais tarde. Levo- **(10)**............ às cinco horas.	
John	Obrigado. Até logo.	

> lhe   lo   o   consigo   lho
> lhe   mim   connosco   nos   me

Grammar in context

The following slogan has been used on leaflets from the Portuguese Animal Protection League, promoting respect for animals. Can you work out what it means?

Porque tu gostas de animais.....

Ajuda-nos a defendê-los!

(Liga Portuguesa dos Direitos do Animal)

18

impersonal verbs

In this unit you will learn
- some impersonal verbs in
  Portuguese, such as those to
  do with the weather, faltar
  and doer

Grammar in focus

Impersonal verbs are those which are found mostly in the third person singular or plural, unless they are being used in a highly literary way. Some are known as 'defective' verbs, as they might not have a full range of tenses. Others may be used with an indirect object pronoun where you would not find one in English. A selection of the most useful follows – add to the list as you come across more, but they are not particularly common.

Weather verbs

There are different ways of talking about the weather in Portuguese, and most phrase and text books cover the topic in full. Some of the common verbs are: **chover** (*to rain*), **nevar** (*to snow*), **chuviscar** (*to drizzle*), **gelar** (*to freeze*), **trovoar** (*to thunder*), as well as various expressions using **fazer** and **haver**.

Na Inglaterra chove mais no Inverno.	*In England it rains more in the winter.*
Está a trovoar.	*It's thundering.*
Faz sol e não há vento.	*It's sunny and there is no wind.*

Anoitecer (to get dark – nightfall) / *amanhecer* (to get light – dawn)

Seria melhor entrar no albergue – está a anoitecer rapidamente.	*It would be better to get into the inn – it's getting dark quickly.*
O dia amanheceu com um sol brilhante.	*The day dawned with a brilliant sun.*

Verbs taking pronouns

To translate *to appeal to / to fancy doing…*, the verb **apetecer** is used with the indirect object pronoun. Hence, *I fancy doing something…* becomes **apetece-me…** + infinitive.

Não nos apetece ver este filme.	*We don't fancy seeing this film.*
Apetece-lhe um passeio de bicicleta?	*Does a bike ride appeal to you?*

Parecer, the verb *to appear* or *seem*, can be used in a similar way to convey a colloquial idea of *to think* – in the sense of *It seems to me…'*

Parecia-me estúpido.	*I thought it was stupid.*
	(It seemed stupid to me.)
É uma boa ideia, não te parece?	*It's a good idea, don't you think?*

Interessar, *to interest*, can be used in exactly the same way – so you can say 'something interests me'.

| Interessou-lhes a venda do barco. | *The sale of the boat interested them.* |
| Não me interessam as mentiras. | *I'm not interested in the lies.* |

Faltar, fazer falta, sobrar

Faltar translates *to be missing, lacking*, and with an indirect pronoun, means *to be short of*.

Faltavam 15 dólares.	*There were 15 dollars missing.*
Falta ar aqui.	*There's a lack of air here.*
Falta-lhes a paciência.	*They are short of patience.*

Fazer falta can mean *to be necessary*, and with a pronoun, *to need / miss*.

| Um martelo faz falta aqui. | *A hammer is needed here.* |
| Não lhes fazia falta a comida inglesa. | *They did not miss English food.* |

Sobrar means *to be more than enough* and *to have left over*.

| Sobra comida, podes comer mais. | *There's more than enough food, you can eat more.* |
| Sobraram-me 20 euros. | *I had 20 euros left over.* |

Doer – when something hurts

To talk about a part of the body hurting in Portuguese, you use **doer** in the singular (if only one part hurts) or the plural (if more than one bit is sore). The indirect object pronoun is also used, so what you are actually saying is 'The ... hurts to me', etc.

Dói-me o braço.	*My arm hurts.*
Doem-lhe os ouvidos.	*His ears (inner ears) hurt.*
Doía-me tanto que tive que me sentar.	*It was hurting me so much that I had to sit down.*

Haver

Unless **haver** is being used in the emphatic expressions illustrated in Unit 30, it only appears in the third person. See also Unit 35.

Há um banco por aqui?	*Is there a bank round here?*
Havia muitos carros parados.	*There were many cars stopped (i.e. stationary).*

Miscellaneous

acontecer	*to happen*
custar	*to cost*
tratar(-se) de	*to be about*
jazer	*to lie* (be laid down) – used for graves in particular

O que aconteceu?	*What has happened?*
Quanto custam as laranjas?	*How much do the oranges cost?*
O filme tratava-se duma mulher em busca do marido.	*The film was about a woman in search of her husband.*
Aqui jaz Álvaro Dionísio Pereira.	*Here lies...*

Exercises

A How would you describe these situations in Portuguese? Choose the correct phrase **a–f**.

1 a boy who still has 5 euros left over after buying some chocolate
2 the gravestone of a beloved creature
3 a snowy penguin scene
4 a price-tag of £10
5 someone who has just been shot in the leg
6 a bike with only one wheel

a Neva muito na Antártica.
b Falta uma roda.
c Sobram-lhe 5 euros.
d Dói-lhe a perna.
e Custa dez libras.
f Aqui jaz o meu sapo favorito.

B Translate the following.

1 No Inverno anoitece mais cedo.
2 I don't fancy going to the party.
3 Que te parece?
4 We are not interested in the money.
5 Faz-me falta a minha namorada.
6 Is there a hospital here?
7 O livro trata duma tragédia.
8 How much does the hat cost?

Grammar in context

This Algarve proverb predicts how long it will keep raining, if it happens to rain on a Sunday, at the time of Mass. How long?

Se chover no Domingo, à hora da Missa, chove a semana inteira.

infinitives

In this unit you will learn
- infinitives of the three verb groups in Portuguese (-ar, -er, -ir)
- about the personal infinitive and its uses

Grammar in focus

The infinitive of a verb in Portuguese is the form that corresponds to the English *to do*, e.g. **falar** = *to speak*. It is the form of the verb you will find in a dictionary, before you manipulate its endings to indicate who is carrying out the action and when (see the following units). In Portuguese, verbs fall into one of three verb groups, known as 'conjugations', depending on whether they end in:

1	-**ar** (the most common)	e.g.	falar	*to speak*
2	-**er**		comer	*to eat*
3	-**ir**		partir	*to leave / break*

There are also a number of irregular verbs which do not belong to these groups, and have peculiarities in their formation (see Units 21, 22, 37 and verb tables).

The general infinitive

Infinitives appear in the following situations:

• After other verb forms, as they might in English.

quero visitar	*I want to visit*
queríamos ir	*we wanted / would like to go*
Deve falar com ela.	*He must (has to) speak with her.*
Não podes fazer isso.	*You cannot (are not able to) do that.*

• After prepositions and verbs taking a preposition, e.g. **gostar de** (*to like*).

Depois de telefonar, ela foi ao trabalho.	*After phoning, she went to work.*
Sempre sonhei em visitar a Grécia.	*I have always dreamed of visiting Greece.*
Fui lá para ver a catedral.	*I went there (in order) to see the cathedral.*

• Impersonally, in expressions such as:

Fumar faz mal.	*Smoking is bad (for you).*
Não é fácil aprender japonês.	*It is not easy to learn Japanese.*

• As an impersonal command form, often on signs in public places.

Sair pela porta traseira!	*Go out through the back door!*
Não fumar aqui.	*No smoking here.*

- As a noun, with the definite article **o**.

  O comer frutas é bom para   *(The) eating (of) fruit is good*
      a saúde.   *for the health.*

The personal infinitive

Portuguese is the only Romance (Latin-based) language which has a personal, or *inflected,* infinitive. As its name suggests, this type of infinitive is personalized – it can be used in its inflected forms (with endings) to refer to whoever is performing the action. It is formed by adding the endings listed below onto the infinitive.

eu (*I*) – no ending	**nós** (*we*) + **mos**
tu (*you*) + **es**	**vós** (*you*) + **des**
ele (*he*) – no ending	**eles** (*they*) + **em**
ela (*she*) – no ending	**elas** (*they*) + **em**
você etc. (*you*) – no ending	**vocês** etc. (*you* plural) + **em**

falar *to speak*		**dizer** *to say*		**partir** *to leave*	
falar	falarmos	dizer	dizermos	partir	partirmos
falares	falardes	dizeres	dizerdes	partires	partirdes
falar	falarem	dizer	dizerem	partir	partirem

Usage

In many cases, the personal infinitive can provide a much simpler alternative to complex constructions, such as those requiring the subjunctive form of the verb (see Units 40–4), and is therefore a valuable linguistic tool. The following are its uses:

- With impersonal expressions

  Não seria melhor tu   *Wouldn't it be better if you left*
      partires já?   *now?*
  É incrível eles estarem cá. *It is incredible that they are*
                              here.

  The meaning of the last example is identical to that of the subjunctive construction:

  É incrível que eles estejam *or* estivessem cá.

- After prepositions.

  Ao termos tentado,   *Having tried / after trying, we*
      conseguimos abrir a porta. *managed to open the door.*
  Não quis continuar sem eles *He did not want to continue*
      aparecerem.   *without them appearing.*

- After prepositional phrases

  These phrases, amongst others, may be followed by the personal infinitive: **antes de** (*before*), **depois de** (*after*), **no caso de** (*in case; if*), **apesar de** (*in spite of*).

Antes de ires embora, escreve o teu novo endereço.	*Before you go away, write down your new address.*
Depois de termos telefonado cinco vezes, o senhor atendeu.	*After we had phoned five times, the man answered.*
No caso de elas chegarem cedo, vou já preparar o quarto.	*In case they arrive early, I'm going to get the bedroom ready now.*
Apesar de vocês cantarem bem, não quero ouvir esta música.	*In spite of your singing well, I don't want to hear this music.*

Distinguishing between verb subjects

The personal infinitive is often used in a sentence describing two separate actions, where there are different subjects for each verb.

Ao **partirem os turistas,** o dono do hotel ficou aliviado.	*When the tourists left, the hotel owner was relieved.*
Antes de **tu viajares,** o carro avariou-se.	*Before you travelled, the car broke down.*

However, it can also be used when the subjects are the same:

Depois de jantarmos no restaurante, ficámos [BP = ficamos] doentes.	*After dining in the restaurant, we became ill.*
Apesar de ter chegado depressa, não pôde ajudar.	*Despite having arrived quickly, he could not help.*
No caso de me sentir mal, ficarei à janela.	*If I feel ill, I'll stay by the window.*

Commands

The personal infinitive is also used with **é favor** as a formal imperative, especially in business contexts (written or spoken), and in public announcements.

É favor enviarem um recibo dentro de um mês.	*Please send a receipt within a month.*
É favor os senhores passageiros não fumarem dentro do vagão.	*Will passengers please refrain from smoking inside the carriage.*

Exercises

A Match the public signs to the correct expressions.

a não nadar
b não virar à esquerda
c não fumar
d não estacionar
e não tirar fotografias
f não entrar
g não deitar lixo
h pagar ao motorista

B Match up the correct ending on to the personal infinitives according to the guidance given. X indicates no additional ending.

Não seria melhor... *Wouldn't it be better...*
1 (tu) comer............   a X
2 (nós) trabalhar............   b -es
3 (ela) visitar............   c -des

4 (eu) abrir............   d X
5 (vocês) estudar............   e X
6 (vós) correr............   f -mos
7 (o Carlos) partir............   g -em
8 (as senhoras) fazer............   h -em

Grammar in context

Both these adverts claim to offer 'the Art of...' (often seen in Tourism). In each case, what is their 'art'?

1

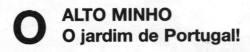

O **ALTO MINHO**
O jardim de Portugal!

NO ALTO MINHO,
RECEBER É UMA ARTE...
A ARTE DE BEM RECEBER!

2

**Restaurante
de interesse Turístico**

A ARTE DE BEM SERVIR

Serviço de Casamentos
e Grupos Turísticos

20

present tense

In this unit you will learn
- how to form the present tense of regular verbs, negatives and questions

Grammar in focus

The indicative mood

This indicates a certain range of verb formations, or endings, for use in most straightforward situations, and is found in a variety of tenses. The subjunctive mood, we shall discover later, is used in other verbal circumstances.

The present tense in Portuguese describes actions or states that are habitual, often with expressions such as **sempre** (*always*), **nunca** (*never*), **cada dia** (*every day*), **às vezes** (*sometimes*), **normalmente** (*normally*) etc. It is also used to describe something that is a fact. It can be used to describe something happening at the time of speech (although in practice other, continuous, tenses are more likely here – see Unit 34), and can convey the (near) future. Therefore,

eu falo can mean *I speak, I am speaking, I do speak, I shall speak*.

First conjugation (-*ar*) verbs

To form the present tense of first conjugation verbs, add the following endings to the stem of the verb. (The stem is the part of the infinitive minus the -**ar** / -**er** / -**ir**.)

falar *to speak*   stem = **fal-**

Singular		Plural	
eu fa**lo**	*I speak*	nós fa**lamos**	*we speak*
tu fa**las**	*you speak*	vós fa**lais**	*you speak*
ele / ela fa**la**	*he / she speaks*	eles / elas fa**lam**	*they speak*
você fa**la**	*you speak*	vocês fa**lam**	*you speak*

A noun, pronoun, or a combination of both, may be used as the subject of the verb. Remember, subject pronouns are only really needed to avoid ambiguity, or for emphasis. Note that the **você** and **vocês** verb forms are the same as the third person singular and plural. The **vós** form (*you plural*) is quite outdated now, and is rarely used apart from in church services and other public addresses, and by older people in rural areas. It is still worth being aware of it, even though you will probably use it very little yourself. To convey 'it...', use the **ele / ela** verb form.

Falo português.	*I speak Portuguese.*
Maria, tu falas francês bem.	*You speak French well, Maria.*
Você fala grego.	*You speak Greek.*

A menina fala devagar.   *The girl speaks slowly.*
A Márcia e eu falamos juntas.   *Marcia and I are speaking*
                                 together.
Os meninos falam na praça.   *The boys talk in the square.*

Negative form

To form the negative of a verb, place **não** directly before it.

Não falo alemão.   *I do not speak German.*
O Pedro não fala bem.   *Pedro does not speak well.*

Interrogative form

To form a simple question, just raise the intonation of your voice at the end of a sentence. Inversion of subject and verb also takes place (the verb is placed before the subject), but not so frequently. The word *do / does* is not translated.

Fala espanhol?   *Do you speak Spanish?*
Falam vocês?   *Do you speak?*

(For more on negatives and interrogatives, refer back to Unit 11.)

Sample verbs of the first conjugation

acabar	to *finish*	parar	to *stop*
fechar	to *close*	regressar	to *return*
ganhar	to *win*	reservar	to *reserve*
gostar (de)	to *like*	saltar	to *jump*
jogar	to *play*	trabalhar	to *work*

Further examples

Eu sempre ando pelo parque.   *I always walk through the*
                               park.
Brincas comigo?   *Will you play with me?*
O filme só começa às oito   *The film only begins at eight.*
  horas.
Não estudamos aos sábados.   *We do not study on Saturdays.*
As amigas jantam em casa   *The friends are dining at home*
  hoje.   *today.*

Second conjugation (*-er*) verbs

comer *to eat*   stem = com-

Singular		Plural	
eu como	*I eat*	nós comemos	*we eat*
tu comes	*you eat*	vós comeis	*you eat*
ele / ela come	*he / she eats*	eles / elas comem	*they eat*
você come	*you eat*	vocês comem	*you eat*

Como peixe.	*I eat fish.*
O João não come carne.	*João does not eat meat.*
Você come batatas?	*Do you eat potatoes?*
Comemos muitos bolos em Portugal.	*We eat a lot of cakes in Portugal.*
Os gatos não comem bem.	*The cats are not eating well.*

Sample verbs of the second conjugation

aprender	*to learn*	fender	*to split, crack*
bater	*to beat*	ofender	*to offend*
comer	*to eat*	responder	*to reply / answer*
debater	*to debate*	vender	*to sell*
escolher	*to choose*	viver	*to live*

Further examples

Não atendo o telefone depois das dez horas da noite.	*I don't answer the phone after ten at night.*
Bebes muito vinho.	*You drink a lot of wine.*
Compreende?	*Do you understand?*
Devemos trabalhar mais.	*We ought to work more.*
Elas escrevem todos os dias.	*They write every day.*

Third conjugation (-*ir*) verbs

partir *to leave* (also *to break / part* in EP)   stem = **part-**

Singular		Plural	
eu parto	*I leave*	nós partimos	*we leave*
tu partes	*you leave*	vós partis	*you leave*
ele / ela parte	*he / she leaves*	eles / elas partem	*they leave*
você parte	*you leave*	vocês partem	*you leave*

Parto no domingo.	*I leave / am leaving on Sunday.*
Já partes?	*Are you leaving already?*
A Ana parte para Londres.	*Ana is leaving for London.*
Eduardo e eu não partimos hoje.	*Eduardo and I are not leaving today.*
Elas partem de avião.	*They leave by plane.*

Sample verbs of the third conjugation

abrir	to open	invadir	to invade
admitir	to admit	omitir	to omit
aplaudir	to applaud	subir	to go up
assistir (a)	to attend	transmitir	to transmit
decidir	to decide	unir	to unite

Further examples

Divido o bolo em quatro.	*I'll divide the cake into four.*
Sempre pedes* dinheiro ao pai.	*You're always asking your Dad for money.*
Você ouve* alguma coisa?	*Can you hear something?*
Dormimos* no mesmo quarto.	*We sleep in the same room.*
Não conseguem* estudar.	*They do not manage to study.*

*All these verbs have an irregularity in the first person form. See Units 21 and 22.

Exercises

A Form the verb in brackets correctly, according to the person carrying out the action.

1 Eu (estudar) geografia e biologia.
2 Nós (comprar) frutas no mercado.
3 Tu não (beber) muita água.
4 Você (responder) às cartas?
5 Ele (abrir) a janela.
6 Vós não (subir) a montanha.
7 Eles (limpar) a casa.
8 Vocês (partir) às três horas?
9 O meu primo (escutar) música clássica.
10 Ela não (comer) carne.

B Complete these sentences by choosing the most appropriate verb from the box, putting the correct ending in each case.

abrir fechar partir chover
servir morar jogar beber
compreender lavar

1 Em Portugal os museus .... às segundas.
2 Ao jantar nós .... água e vinho.
3 O empregado .... os cafés ao terraço.
4 Eu .... numa casa antiga.

5 Não .... muito no interior do Brasil.
6 Vocês .... a mala, por favor?
7 Tu .... futebol todos os dias.
8 Vós todos .... inglês?
9 A que horas é que você ....?
10 Elas .... o carro do pai.

Grammar in context

Read the following text about the northern Portuguese town of
Penafiel, and answer the questions about it.

Rica de história, Penafiel é
igualmente uma rica região
rural e de florescente e
diversificado comércio, ao
mesmo tempo que sede de
importantes empresas
industriais. O seu granito,
sob a forma de guias para
passeios, pavimentos ou
cantaria, cobre as ruas e
enriquece a arquitectura de
muitas cidades do mundo
(quem sabe se também da
sua...). Também o Vinho
Verde da região é famoso e
serve-se à mesa dos
principais restaurantes.

1 In what kind of a region is Penafiel set?
2 Of what type of stone is much of the city made?
3 What famous wine is served in the best restaurants?
4 There are four examples of -er verbs in the text – can you
   spot them? Their meanings are: *cover*, *enrich*, *know*, *serve*.

21

radical-changing verbs

In this unit you will learn
- the most common radical-changing verbs – those that change their spelling in the stem (radical)

Grammar in focus

A number of verbs in Portuguese change their spelling slightly in the present indicative tense. The change occurs in the stem, or radical, of the verb in all persons except the **nós** and **vós** forms. Since the present subjunctive (see Unit 40) is based on the first person singular of the present indicative, its correct spelling is a vital starting point for the formation of the subjunctive.

Here are some of the more common types of radical-changing verbs.

First conjugation, -ar

boiar, *to float*
bóio, bóias, bóia, boiamos, boiais, **bóiam**
A written accent is added.

recear, *to fear / be afraid of*
receio, receias, receia, receamos, receais, **receiam**
An **i** is added.

odiar, *to hate*
odeio, odeias, odeia, odiamos, odiais, **odeiam**
An **e** is added.

Other verbs similar to **odiar** include: **incendiar** (*to set fire to*), **negociar** (*to negotiate*) and **premiar** (*to reward*).

Second conjugation, -er

erguer, *to rise*
ergo, ergues, ergue, erguemos, ergueis, erguem
Irregular only in the first person singular.

Third conjugation, -ir

The majority of changes occur in these verbs. The changes take place in the first person singular only, and therefore carry over to the present subjunctive.

- e changes to i

conseguir	*to achieve / manage*	consigo	*I manage*
divertir	*to enjoy*	divirto	*I enjoy*
mentir	*to lie*	minto	*I lie*
repetir	*to repeat*	repito	*I repeat*
seguir	*to follow*	sigo	*I follow*

sentir	to *feel*	sinto	*I feel*
servir	to *serve*	sirvo	*I serve*
vestir	to *dress*	visto	*I dress*

- o changes to u

cobrir	to *cover*	cubro	*I cover*
descobrir	to *discover*	descubro	*I discover*
dormir	to *sleep*	durmo	*I sleep*

polir, *to polish* becomes: pulo, pules, pule, polimos, polis, pulem

- u changes to o
subir, *to go up* changes thus: subo, sobes, sobe, subimos, subis, sobem

Exercises

A Complete the table by writing in the correct forms of the verbs.

recear	1 eu	tu receias	2 o Paulo	nós	vós	eles
	......		......	receamos	receais	receiam
divertir	divirto	3	diverte	divertimos	4	divertem
5	sinto	sentes	sente	6	sentis	sentem
dormir	7	dormes	dorme	dormimos	dormis	8 ......
subir	subo	9	sobe	10	subis	sobem
11	odeias	odeia	12	odiamos	odiais	odeiam

B Translate the following:

1 Are you (**tu**) afraid of the exam?
2 We hate the winter.
3 I can't (manage to) eat more.
4 He's lying.
5 Can you (**vós**) repeat the phrase?
6 They (**elas**) cover the child.
7 I discover the secret.
8 Are you (**tu**) coming up?

o exame	*exam*	**mais**	*more*
a frase	*phrase*	**a criança**	*child*
o segredo	*secret*		

Grammar in context

Casa da Anta
Hotel Rural

LANHELAS MINHO NORTE DE PORTUGAL

Descubra o verdadeiro charme do Minho.

As suas lindas montanhas e rios, a sua cozinha regional, os mercados
locais, os festivais populares, o seu folclore e o calor da sua gente,
fazem do Minho uma deliciosa escolha para as suas férias.

CONTACTE COM A NATUREZA

Acampe e divirta-se no nosso parque em Vilar do Mouros

1 What are you invited to discover?
2 Where are you invited to enjoy yourself?

22

orthographic-changing verbs

In this unit you will learn
- the most common orthographic-changing verbs – those that modify their spelling for reasons of pronunciation

Grammar in focus

Orthographic-changing verbs are those which require a slight modification in their spelling (orthography) in order to maintain correct pronunciation. The spelling change takes place on the last consonant of the stem of the verb before certain vowels, as listed below. The most common changes are as follows:

- Verbs ending in -car
  Before an e the c changes to **qu**, to maintain a hard c sound.

  ficar, *to stay*: fico *I stay*, fiquei *I stayed*

  Other verbs of this type are:

acercar-se	to *approach*
brincar	to *play*
colocar	to *place*
explicar	to *explain*
indicar	to *indicate*
modificar	to *modify*
multiplicar	to *multiply*
publicar	to *publish*
sacar	to *remove*
tocar	to *touch / play* (instrument)

- Verbs ending in -çar

  Before e, the ç changes to c, as the cedilla is no longer required to maintain a soft c sound.

  caçar, *to hunt*: caço *I hunt*, cacei *I hunted*

  Other verbs of this type are:

almoçar	to *have lunch*
ameaçar	to *threaten*
calçar	to *put on / take a certain size in shoes / gloves*
começar	to *begin*

- Verbs ending in -gar

  Before e, the g becomes **gu** to maintain the hard g sound.

  chegar, *to arrive*: chego *I arrive*, cheguei *I arrived*

  Other verbs of this type are:

apagar	to *extinguish*
entregar	to *hand over*
jogar	to *play*
julgar	to *judge*

obrigar   to *compel / oblige*
pagar   to *pay*
prolongar to *prolong*

- Verbs ending in -cer

Before a or o, the c becomes ç to maintain the soft c (s) sound.

conhecer, to *know*: conheço I *know*, conhece he *knows*

Other verbs of this type include:

acontecer to *happen*
agradecer to *thank*
aquecer   to *heat*
descer   to *descend*
esquecer   to *forget*
merecer   to *deserve*
obedecer   to *obey*
parecer   to *seem / appear*
reconhecer to *recognize*

- Verbs ending in -ger and -gir

Before a or o, the g becomes j to maintain the soft g sound.

fugir, to *flee*: fujo I *flee*, foge he *flees*

Other verbs of this type are:

abranger   to *include / comprise*
afligir   to *afflict / distress*
corrigir   to *correct*
dirigir (BP) to *drive / direct*
eleger   to *elect / choose*
exigir   to *demand / require*
fingir   to *pretend*
proteger   to *protect*

- Verbs ending in -guer and -guir

Before a or o, gu simply becomes g to maintain the hard g sound.

seguir to *follow*: sigo I *follow*, segue he *follows*

Other verbs of this type are:

conseguir to *achieve / obtain / succeed*
distinguir to *distinguish*
erguer   to *erect*
perseguir to *pursue / persecute*

You will also come across examples of far rarer verbs whose orthography changes. The best thing to do when you meet them is to make a special note, but if you are not likely to want to make real active use of them yourself, don't lose sleep over them.

Exercises

A Choose the correct verb form from a choice of three, to match the underlined word in each phrase.

		a	**b**	**c**
1	I <u>placed</u>	coloquei	colocei	coloco
2	You (**tu**) <u>wear</u> size 36 shoes.	calcas	calça	calças
3	He <u>plays</u> football.	joge	joga	jogua
4	We <u>heat</u> the water.	aquecemos	acecemos	aqecemos
5	They <u>protect</u> the house.	protejem	proteguem	protegem
6	I <u>follow</u> them.	siguo	sigo	sijo
7	I <u>didn't</u> <u>touch</u> the vase.	não toquei	não tocei	não toque
8	<u>Did</u> you (**tu**) <u>begin</u> the work?	começas	começaste	comecaste
9	Ana <u>paid</u> the bill.	pagou	pago	paguo
10	They <u>obey</u> the teacher.	obedeçem	obedequem	obedecem

B Match the correct response to each question.

1 Consegues fazer o exercício?	**a** O João dirige.
	b Cheguei às nove.
2 Quem dirige o carro?	**c** Começámos às três.
3 Descem aqui?	**d** Apaguei.
4 A que horas chegou você?	**e** Consigo.
5 A que horas almoçam aqueles senhores?	**f** Eles protegem.
	g Brinquei.
6 Brincaste com a bola?	**h** Descemos, sim.
7 Que instrumento tocas?	**i** Toco o piano.
8 Quando começaram o trabalho?	**j** Almoçam ao 12.30.
9 Apagou o fogo?	
10 Quem protege a casa?	

Grammar in context

★ Pague 1, Leve 2! ★

What do you think this offer means?

23

reflexive verbs

In this unit you will learn
- how to form reflexive verbs
  (*I wash myself*) in
  Portuguese
- about the position of the
  reflexive pronoun in the
  sentence

Grammar in focus

A reflexive verb is used where the subject and object of the action are the same person or thing, with the subject acting upon itself. To express this, the verb is used with a reflexive pronoun (look back at Unit 17). The dictionary will indicate that a verb is reflexive, by adding the pronoun -se (*self*) after it.

sentar-se, *to sit (oneself) down*
present tense: *I sit (myself) down, you sit (yourself) down, etc.*

sento-**me**	sentamo-**nos***
sentas-**te**	sentais-**vos**
senta-**se**	sentam-**se**

Sentas-te aqui?	*Are you sitting here?*
Os alunos sentam-se sem falar.	*The pupils sit down without talking.*

lavar-se, *to wash oneself*

preterite tense (see Unit 25): *I washed myself, you washed yourself, etc.*

lavei-**me**	lavámo-**nos***
lavaste-**te**	lavastes-**vos**
lavou-**se**	lavaram-**se**

Lavou-se depois do trabalho.	*He got (himself) washed after work.*
Lavei-me bem.	*I had a good wash* (washed myself well).

*With the reflexive pronoun, the s is dropped from the verb form of the first person plural when the pronoun follows the verb.

Position of the reflexive pronoun

In Portugal, the normal position for the pronoun is at the end of the verb, joined to it by a hyphen. In Brazil the reflexive pronoun commonly appears before the verb. In both countries the pronoun precedes the verb in negative statements, with questions, and in other circumstances detailed in Unit 17.

Levanto-me às sete e meia.	*I get (myself) up at 7.30.*
[BP] Eu me chamo Cafu.	*I'm called Cafu.* (I call myself)
Ela nunca se senta comigo.	*She never sits with me.*
Com que te lavaste?	*What did you wash yourself with?*

Although some verbs, like **atrever-se** (*to dare*), are always used in the reflexive, others serve a dual purpose, depending on whether they are used with the reflexive pronoun or not.

chamar	*to call*	chamar-se	*to be called*
cortar	*to cut*	cortar-se	*to cut oneself*
deitar	*to throw down*	deitar-se	*to lie down, go to bed*
lavar	*to wash*	lavar-se	*to have a wash*
levantar	*to lift up, raise*	levantar-se	*to get up, rise*
sentir	*to sense, suffer*	sentir-se	*to feel, consider oneself*

In fact, you will find that many verbs can be made reflexive in the same way, if you want the action to be carried out both by and to the subject of the verb.

Reciprocity

The reflexive pronoun may also be used when there is an interaction between plural subjects of a verb; the subjects carry out the action on each other.

Vemo-**nos** todos os dias.   *We see each other every day.*

Sometimes, ambiguity about the true meaning, reflexive or reciprocal, may emerge, such as in:

felicitaram-se = *they congratulated themselves or they congratulated each other.*

In order to avoid this problem, the following additions may be useful.

um ao outro / uma à outra	*(to) one another, each other*
uns aos outros / umas às outras	*(to) one another (plural)*
mutuamente	*mutually*
Felicitaram-se **um ao outro**.	*They congratulated each other.*
Adoram-se mutuamente.	*They adore each other.*

Exercises

A Decide what is happening in each picture and correctly form the verbs in the present tense for the people involved.

1  Eu ....

2 Tu ....

3 O Miguel ....

4 Nós ....

5

Como é que você ....?

6 Eu ....

7 Elas ....

8   Tu ....

9   Ela não ....

10   Vocês ....

B Supply the correct reflexive pronoun in each sentence, deciding also where the pronoun should be placed (assume standard European positions).

1 Tu não .... levantas .... cedo.
2 Ela .... senta .... no sofá.
3 Eu .... esqueci .... do livro.
4 O João .... veste .... lentamente.
5 Nós nunca .... encontramos .... à hora certa.
6 Elas .... deitam .... depois do jantar.
7 Eu ainda não .... vesti ....
8 Como .... chama .... o teu amigo?
9 Ninguém .... lembra .... da festa.
10 Já .... lavaram .... ?

Language watch 4

Words ending in **-ável** in Portuguese usually correspond to -*able* in English (and French and Spanish, if you are already a student of those languages too). Similarly, the ending **-ível** corresponds to -*ible*.

Portuguese	Spanish	French	English
razoável	razonable	raisonnable	reasonable
admirável	admirable	admirable	admirable
responsável	responsable	responsable	responsible
respeitável	respetable	respectable	respectable
considerável	considerable	considérable	considerable
comestível	comestible	comestible	edible
(comer = *to eat* in Portuguese and Spanish)			
legível	legible	lisible	legible
suscetível	susceptible	susceptible	susceptible / sensitive

24

verbs followed by a preposition

In this unit you will learn
- about verbs followed by prepositions in Portuguese

Grammar in focus

Some verbs require a preposition after them when used before an infinitive. The equivalent English verbs do not always require a preposition, and, when they do, the preposition does not necessarily correspond with the one used in Portuguese. A number of the examples below are commonly used verbs, so you will soon get used to them; for others, which you will learn only when you come across them, it may be worth forming your own group lists as set out below, and constantly looking over them and adding to them as you go along.

Verbs + *a*

acostumar-se a	*to get used to*
aprender a	*to learn how to*
atrever-se a	*to dare to*
começar a	*to begin to*
decidir-se a	*to decide to*
forçar a	*to force to*
levar a	*to cause to*
meter-se a	*to set out to*
obrigar a	*to oblige to*
ocupar-se a	*to busy oneself with*
pôr-se a	*to start*
resignar-se a	*to resign oneself to*

Nunca me acostumei ao calor aqui.
I've never got used to the heat here.
Decidiram-se a voltar.
They decided to turn back.
Ele vai ocupar-se a cortar a relva.
He's going to be busy cutting the lawn.

Verbs + *de*

acusar de	*to accuse of*
arrepender-se de	*to repent*
deixar de	*to stop*
dissuadir de	*to dissuade from*
encarregar-se de	*to undertake*
esquecer-se de	*to forget to*
fartar-se de	*to get tired of, to do something to excess*
gostar de	*to like*
impedir de	*to prevent from*
lembrar-se de	*to remember to*

parar de	*to stop*
precisar de	*to need to*

Você precisa de descansar.	*You need to rest.*
Impediram o Tó de abrir a porta.	*They prevented Tó from opening the door.*
Ninguém vai se encarregar de comprar os bilhetes.	*Nobody's going to be in charge of buying* (undertake to buy) *the tickets.*

Verbs + *em*

concordar em	*to agree to*
consistir em	*to consist of*
fazer bem em	*to do well to*
fazer mal em	*to do wrong to*
insistir em	*to insist on*
pensar em	*to think of*
vacilar em, hesitar em	*to hesitate to*

O trabalho consiste em limpar a casa e preparar a comida.	*The work consists of cleaning the house and preparing the food.*
Fazes mal em pensar assim.	*You do wrong to think like that.*
Pensava em fugir.	*He thought about running away.*

Verbs + *por*

acabar por	*to end up*
começar por	*to begin by*
esforçar-se por	*to make an effort to*
lutar por	*to fight to*
principiar por	*to begin by*
suspirar por	*to long to*
terminar por	*to end by*

Acabaram por ficar a noite intcira.	*They ended up staying the whole night.*
Terminou por agradecer todos os ouvintes.	*She finished by thanking all the listeners.*
Vou começar por dizer...	*I'm going to begin by saying...*

Verbs + *com* / *para*

contar com	*to count on*	preparar-se para	*to prepare to*
sonhar com	*to dream of*	servir para	*to serve to*

Não pode contar com ganhar o dinheiro.
You can't count on winning the money.

Sempre sonhavam com morar no campo.
They always dreamed of living in the country.

Os soldados prepararam-se para lutar.
The soldiers prepared to fight.

Isto serve para nos dizer alguma coisa.
This serves to tell us something.

Some of these verbs are also used with their preposition when followed by a noun. In these cases, when the articles (definite and indefinite) are present, you must remember to combine them with the preposition, according to the rules of contraction, e.g. **do, das, dumas** etc. (Refer back to Unit 2.)

Ela resignou-se ao trabalho.
She resigned herself to the work.

Lembraste-te do pão?
Have you remembered the bread?

Nunca vamos concordar nisto.
We're never going to agree on this.

Tem de lutar pela pátria.
You have to fight for your homeland.

Sonho com pastéis de nata!
I dream of (Portuguese) custard cakes!

Preparavam-se para o jantar.
They were getting ready for dinner.

Exercises

A Match the English and Portuguese verbs, and decide which preposition follows each one.

1	to get used to	**a**	concordar+?
2	to force to	**b**	sonhar+?
3	to agree to	**c**	acabar+?
4	to end up (...ing)	**d**	servir+?
5	to count on	**e**	fazer mal+?
6	to prepare to	**f**	forçar+?
7	to learn how to	**g**	preparar-se+?
8	to stop (...ing)	**h**	contar+?

9 to do wrong to   i acostumar-se+?
10 to fight to   j deixar+?
11 to dream of   k aprender+?
12 to serve to / for   l lutar+?

B Translate the following:

1 Ana was learning how to drive.
2 You do right to complain; it's far too expensive.
3 This situation serves to illustrate the difficulties of living in a foreign country.
4 The fight caused me to stay at home for two weeks.
5 The men were prevented from moving any nearer.
6 My brother always longed to travel the world.

to drive	**conduzir [BP = dirigir]**
to complain	**reclamar**
to illustrate	**ilustrar / exemplificar**
foreign country	**um país estrangeiro**
to move nearer	**aproximar-se**
to travel the world	**viajar pelo mundo**

Grammar in context

After a disastrous footballing defeat at the hands of Finland, the Portuguese national team bounced back with a better game against Brazil. This is how one team member, Sérgio Conceição, described the improvement:

Brasil serviu para limpar imagem com a Finlândia

serviu = past tense (*served*)

Can you guess what his feelings were?

25

preterite tense

In this unit you will learn
- how to talk about past actions with the preterite tense

Grammar in focus

This tense serves the purpose of expressing past action that is completed. It is also used to translate *have done* (but see also Unit 32). It is formed by adding these endings to the *stem* (the first part of the infinitive, minus the -ar / -er / -ir).

	-ar verbs	*-er* verbs	*-ir* verbs
eu	+ ei	+ i	+ i
tu	+ aste	+ este	+ iste
ele / ela / você	+ ou	+ eu	+ iu
nós	+ ámos [BP = amos]	+ emos	+ imos
vós	+ astes	+ estes	+ istes
eles / elas / vocês	+ aram	+ eram	+ iram

First conjugation (-ar) verbs

falar *spoke, did speak, have spoken*
falei   falámos
falaste   falastes
falou   falaram

Ontem falei com a minha tia.	*Yesterday I spoke with my aunt.*
Ainda não preparaste o jantar?	*Have you not prepared dinner yet?*
O marido dela pagou tudo.	*Her husband paid for everything.*
Comprámos aquela casa bonita.	*We have bought that beautiful house.*
As filhas limparam o quintal.	*The daughters cleaned the back garden.*

Second conjugation (-er) verbs

comer *ate, did eat, have eaten*
comi   comemos
comeste   comestes
comeu   comeram

Não comi o peixe.	*I did not eat the fish.*
Vendeste o nosso carro?	*Have you sold our car?*
Você já bebeu suficiente.	*You have drunk enough now.*
O ano passado escrevemos muitas cartas.	*Last year we wrote many letters.*
Eles não leram a mensagem.	*They did not read the message.*

Third conjugation (-*ir*) verbs

partir *left, did leave, have left, broke, etc.*

parti	partimos
partiste	partistes
partiu	partiram

Só parti depois do almoço.	*I only left after lunch.*
Porque não abriste a prenda?	*Why haven't you opened the present?*
Ela ouviu um barulho estranho.	*She heard a strange noise.*
Mentimos, mas não muito!	*We lied, but not much!*
Vocês sentiram alguma coisa?	*Did you feel / hear something / anything?*

You should be able to see patterns forming which can help you to learn these endings, e.g.

falaste	comeste	partiste
falámos	comemos	partimos

Each verb here maintains the original letter it had in the infinitive (**a** / **e** / **i**).

The *we* (**nós**) forms for **-er** and **-ir** verbs are the same as in the present tense (as is also the **-ar** form in Brazil, with no written accent). It is therefore important to look for clues to tell you which tense the verb is in – look for words defining time, e.g. *yesterday, last week, today* etc.

Don't see these as a frightening array of new forms to memorize; make the patterns work to help you minimize your learning effort. Irregular verbs have irregular forms in the past tense too. See Unit 37 and the verb tables on pages 263–71.

Some examples of irregular verbs

Fiz um bolo para a festa. [fazer]	*I made a cake for the party.*
Onde foste? [ir]	*Where have you been? / Where did you go?*
Ela não viu nada. [ver]	*She did not see anything.*
Tivemos muita sorte. [ter]	*We were very lucky.*
Vieram com os pais. [vir]	*They came with their parents.*

Exercises

A Convert the verbs in italics in the present tense to the preterite, then re-order the sentences to tell the story of a day at a football match. Some of them have been done for you to help you sort it out.

1 *Chego* ao estádio às duas e meia.

2 *Bebo* uma Coca Cola.
6 bebi

3 Ao meio tempo *como* um hambúrguer.

4 O Ipswich *transforma* o pénalti.

5 O Ipswich *ganha* 3–0.

6 *Apanho* [BP = pego] o autocarro [BP = o ônibus].

7 *Compro* um programa.

8 O Ipswich *marca* um golo [BP = gol].
8 marcou

9 O Manchester *comete* uma falta na área de pénalti.

10 O Ipswich *marca* um terceiro golo/gol.
14 marcou

11 *Saio* de casa às duas. **1 saí**

12 *Compro* um bilhete.

13 *Encontro* o meu lugar.

14 *Vou* ao meu lugar outra vez. **10 fui**

15 O árbitro *expulsa* um jogador do Manchester.

16 Os aficionados *estão* loucos com alegria.
16 estiveram

chegar	to arrive	**marcar um golo / gol**	to score a goal
beber	to drink	**cometer**	to commit
comer	to eat	**sair**	to go out / leave
		transformar o pénalti	to get the penalty
ganhar	to win	**encontrar**	to find
apanhar	to catch	**ir (vou)**	to go
comprar	to buy	**expulsar**	to send off

B Translate these verbs into Portuguese and complete the puzzle with them.

1 they found
2 you (**tu**) paid
3 you (plural) opened
4 I've spoken
5 they've bought
6 we spoke
7 he touched
8 you (sing. polite) read (past)

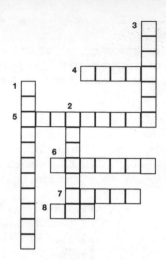

Grammar in context

Read this conversation about someone's recent holiday, and fill in the details on the grid about what they did.

A Então, gostou da visita?
B Gostei imenso. Adorei a região e a comida.
A Onde visitou?
B Pois, chegámos na terça-feira, e na quarta visitámos uma quinta de Vinho Verde. Provámos o vinho e depois passeiámos de barco no rio.
A Foram num passeio de comboio [BP = trem]?
B Bem, o meu marido apanhou um comboio histórico no sábado, e foi até Pinhão. Eu fiquei na cidade e explorei a pé.
A Onde ficaram hospedados?
B Ficámos num pequeno hotel, uma residencial, no centro de Vila Real, e voltámos lá todos os dias.
A E a comida?
B Pois, comemos os pratos típicos da região. O meu marido adorou a truta, mas eu preferi os doces.

When did they arrive?	
What did they do on the Wednesday?	
What did the husband do on the Saturday?	
Where did they stay?	
What food did she like?	

26

imperfect tense

In this unit you will learn
- how to form and use the imperfect tense to talk about continuous actions, habits and states in the past

Grammar in focus

This tense is used to express an action which was happening in the past, something continuous, as well as for repeated or habitual actions. It is used as description, especially for the background to a story or event that is being narrated. It has a variety of other uses, which are explained below.

It is formed by adding the following endings to the stem of the verb:

	-*ar* verbs	-*er* verbs	-*ir* verbs
eu	+ ava	+ ia	+ ia
tu	+ avas	+ ias	+ ias
ele / ela / você	+ ava	+ ia	+ ia
nós	+ ávamos	+ íamos	+ íamos
vós	+ áveis	+ íeis	+ íeis
eles / elas / vocês	+ avam	+ iam	+ iam

You will see that the -**er** and -**ir** verbs have identical endings. See Unit 37 for the imperfect of the irregular verbs **ser** and **ter**.

Usage

- Incomplete, unfinished actions or states in the past, often happening at the time a finished action took place and interrupted them.

  Chovia muito e o vento estava forte quando chegaram. | *It was raining heavily and the wind was strong when they arrived.*

- Actions going on simultaneously in the past.

  Enquanto ela fazia o jantar, o marido lia o jornal. | *Whilst she was making dinner, her husband was reading the paper.*

  However, the two types of situation above are more often conveyed through the use of a continuous tense (see Unit 34).

- Repeated or habitual actions in the past – often translated in English by *used to....* .

  Durante as férias passávamos todos os dias na praia. | *During the holidays we used to spend every day on the beach.*

  Quando eram pequenos, moravam no campo. | *When they were little they lived (used to live) in the country.*

Quando voltava da escola, sempre brincava depois de fazer os deveres da casa.

When I got home (used to get home) from school, I would always play after doing my work.

- As a colloquial substitute in EP for the conditional tense (see Unit 29).

Gostava de ir ao cinema.

I would like to go to the cinema [conditional = **gostaria**].

- In polite statements and requests, often in place of the conditional.

Podia dizer-me as horas, por favor?

Could you tell me the time, please?

Queríamos dois cafés, se faz favor.

We would like two coffees, please.

- The verb **costumar** (*to be accustomed to*) is used in the imperfect as a means to express habitual action in the past, especially when compared with what happens now in the present.

Ela costumava ir a pé ao trabalho; agora apanha [BP = pega] o autocarro [BP = ônibus].

She used to walk to work; now she catches the bus.

Quando morávamos em Londres, nunca costumávamos sair.

When we lived in London we never used to go out.

- The imperfect tense is also used to denote age and time in the past.

O José só tinha oito anos quando foi viver ao Brasil.

José was only eight when he went to live in Brazil.

Que horas eram quando te vi?   Eram dez e meia.

What time was it when I saw you?   It was 10.30.

Exercises

A Edu is looking through his photo album from when he was a young boy. For each of his thoughts, put the action of the verb in the infinitive into the imperfect, and complete each sentence by choosing an appropriate phrase from the box.

1 I used to live (**viver**) in the countryside.
2 I used to play (**jogar**) football every day.
3 I didn't used to go (**frequentar**) to school much.
4 I used to read (**ler**) in the garden.
5 I used to help (**ajudar**) at home.
6 I used to go out (**sair**) with friends.
7 I used to make (**fazer**) cakes with my mother.
8 I used to go (**ir**) to church on Sundays.

> a escola muito   com amigos
> à igreja aos domingos   no campo
> no jardim   bolos com a mãe
> futebol todos os dias   em casa

B Supply the correct form of each verb in these examples.

1 (Você) .... (poder) dizer-me onde fica o banco, se faz favor?
2 (Nós) .... (querer) dois cafés, por favor.
3 (Vocês) .... -me (dizer) as horas, por favor?
4 O que (tu) .... (gostar) de fazer amanhã?
5 (Eu) .... (ir) ao concerto, mas tenho muito trabalho.
6 Quantos anos é que (você) .... (ter) quando aprendeu a conduzir [BP = dirigir]?
7 .... (ser) dez horas quando o gerente chegou.
8 Enquanto tu .... (estudar), nós .... (lavar) o carro.
9 (Eles) .... (costumar) tocar piano.
10 A Sónia .... (comer) peixe todos os dias.

Grammar in context

Look at this adapted extract from **O Principezinho** (*The Little Prince*), and see if you can spot the verbs in the imperfect. Work out a list of infinitives for those you find, and find out what they mean in English.

O quinto planeta era extremamente curioso. Era o mais pequeno de todos. Só lá havia espaço, à justa, para um candeeiro e um acendedor de candeeiros. O principezinho olhava e olhava e pensava profundamente, mas por muitas voltas que desse à cabeça, não conseguia perceber para que é que podiam servir, algures no espaço, num planeta que não tinha nem casas nem população, um candeeiro e um acendedor de candeeiros.

[From: Antoine de Saint-Exupéry, *The Little Prince*, translated into Portuguese by Joana Morais Varela]

Imperfect	Infinitive	English
e.g. era	ser	*to be*

27

preterite vs. imperfect

In this unit you will learn
- how to decide between the preterite and the imperfect when talking about the past
- how to say that one event interrupted another

Grammar in focus

It is sometimes a difficult decision as to which of these two tenses to use when talking about the past. In summary, it may be useful to remember that:

- The **imperfect** conveys an action or state which has a certain amount of continuity to it, without the time constriction of a beginning or an end, or is used for an action which may be repeated a number of times, again with no limitation of time.

- The **preterite** is linked much more closely with time limits, and is used with completed actions in the past, often with references to particular times or periods. A specific start or finish to the action may be expressed. It also translates the English perfect tense, as in

Falaste com ela? *Have you spoken to her?*

Imperfect

PAST   NOW   >>>

Enquanto eu lia um livro, ela ouvia música.
Whilst I was reading a book, she was listening to music.

Fazia muito sol quando partimos para as férias.
It was very sunny when we left for our holidays.

Antigamente, o Rui cantava nos bares de Lisboa.
In the past Rui used to sing in the bars of Lisbon.

Preterite

PAST   NOW   >>>

A minha prima cortou a perna. *My cousin cut her leg.*

Estive no jardim, e tu?
I've been in the garden, and you?

O ano passado passámos uma semana em Minas Gerais.
Last year we spent a week in Minas Gerais.

Although the rules above may help in many situations, it must be said that sometimes the distinction between the two tenses is more blurred, requiring you to consider much more carefully the situation / action you wish to describe. If you read widely in the language, particularly good newspapers and magazines, you will start to build up a better picture of how these tenses are commonly used. A few further examples follow.

- *I was very sad when I saw the film.*

Estava muito triste quando vi o filme.	= I was already sad when I saw it.
Fiquei muito triste quando...	= I became sad as a result of seeing it.

- *It was not easy to read.*

Não **era** fácil de ler.	= It was not an easy document to read, irrespective of when it might be read.
Não **foi** fácil de ler.	= At that particular time it proved difficult to read.

- *She got up at eight.*

Levantava-se às oito (todos os dias).	= This was her habit – what she used to do.
Levantou-se às oito.	= seen over a limited space of time, e.g. yesterday

Onde **estavam** quando telefonei?	= *Where were you* (at the point in time) *when I phoned?* (no time limits)
Onde **estiveram** ontem?	= *Where were you yesterday?* (time limit of yesterday imposed, therefore the day is seen as a whole point in time)

Vivia em Londres (em 1997).	= *He was living in London* (during 1997). / *He used to live in London* (without a time reference). This was an on-going action during that particular span of time.
Viveu em Londres em 1997.	= *He lived in London in 1997.* The action of being in London is seen as a completed action for the time span of that year. It is likely he moved elsewhere after this point.

- Não **conhecia** o teu irmão. = *I didn't know your brother.* (Time had not yet brought his acquaintance.)

  Só o **conheci** na festa. = *I only got to know him at the party.* (Acquaintance came about at a single event.)

Estar a fazer

To convey an action going on in the past, especially when related to a specific event interrupting it, use the imperfect of **estar** (*to be*), plus **a**, plus the infinitive of the verb (the action in progress). This is known as a progressive, or continuous tense, and is widely used in Portuguese. In Brazil the formation is imperfect of **estar**, plus the gerund of the verb – the part of a verb ending in **-ando** / **-endo** / **-indo** (the *-ing* part). See also Units 31 and 34.

Estava a tomar banho quando o telefone tocou.	*I was having a bath when the phone rang.*
Estavam a dormir quando chegámos.	*They were sleeping when we arrived.*
Que estava fazendo às nove horas?	*What were you doing at nine o'clock?*
Estava vendo a televisão.	*I was watching TV.*
Quando saímos, estava a chover.	*When we left it was raining.* (It was already raining at that point.)
Quando saímos, choveu.	*When we left it rained.* (It started to rain at that point.)

Exercises

A Match up the Portuguese sentences with the corresponding English versions.

1 Eu estava a ver um bom filme.

2 Começou a chover esta manhã.

3 O Miguel tomava duche todos os dias.

4 Ela leu o livro, depois saiu.

5 Ela estava a ler o livro às três horas.

6 Eles viviam em São Paulo.

a Miguel had a shower every day.

b She was reading her book at three o'clock.

c They were living in São Paulo when I got to know them.

d We were working, and you?

e It started raining this morning.

7 Estávamos trabalhando, e tu?
8 Eles viviam em São Paulo quando os conheci.
9 O que estavas a fazer?
10 Eles viveram em São Paulo só dois anos.

f They only lived in São Paulo for two years.
g What were you doing?
h I was watching a good film.
i They used to live in São Paulo.
j She read the book, then went out.

B Decide whether the correct tense (underlined) has been used in each sentence. Remember that in some situations, either one can be valid depending on the viewpoint and time reference. Correct the ones you think are incorrect.

1 O António não <u>estava</u> em casa quando <u>fomos</u> lá.
2 Quando ela <u>chegou</u>, os outros <u>estavam</u> a trabalhar.
3 O que é que fez ontem? <u>Ia</u> ao centro.
4 Quando encontrei o meu amigo, ele <u>vestiu-se</u> de preto.
5 <u>Vivíamos</u> lá há dois anos.
6 Quando você era pequena, <u>estava a sair</u> muito?
7 <u>Falaram</u> com ele no sábado.
8 Eu <u>atendia</u> o telefone quando tocou.
9 O sr. Silva <u>estava pintando</u> a casa em duas horas.
10 Na escola sempre <u>ouvíamos</u> música todos os dias.

C Complete the table with the appropriate verb forms.

	hoje	a semana passada	antigamente
eu	falo	falei	falava
ele	vende	....	....
vocês	....	partiram	....
tu	....	....	compravas
nós	comemos	....	....
elas	....	abriram	....
eu	....	....	fazia
ela	tem	....	....

Grammar in context

Look at this advert for an interactive Brazilian history reference product.

> VOCÊ VAI ENTENDER COMO
> CABRAL DESCOBRIU O BRASIL.
> VOCÊ VAI ENTENDER COMO
> D. PEDRO I PROCLAMOU A
> INDEPENDÊNCIA. VOCÊ VAI
> ENTENDER INCLUSIVE COMO É
> QUE ESSE DINHEIRINHO QUE
> VOCÊ RECEBE JÁ MUDOU
> TANTO DE NOME.

1 What two historical events does it say you can learn about?
2 What can you learn about the money you earn?

28

future tense

In this unit you will learn
- the formation and use of the future tense in Portuguese

Grammar in focus

The future tense expresses action that has not yet happened. In English we use *will* or *shall* to convey the future. The future tense is used less in Portuguese than in English, as it is often substituted by the present tense, especially in the spoken language. The endings for the future tense in Portuguese are quite straightforward: there is just one set of endings for all verbs, which are added on to the infinitive of the verb. There are three verbs with irregular spelling changes.

The future is formed by adding the following endings to the infinitive of all verbs:

	all verbs
eu	+ ei
tu	+ ás
ele / ela / você	+ á
nós	+ emos
vós	+ eis
eles / elas / vocês	+ ão

The three irregulars are: **dizer** (*to say*), which becomes **dir** + endings, **fazer** (*to do / make*), which becomes **far** + endings, and **trazer** (*to bring*), becoming **trar** + endings.

Passarei as férias a trabalhar.	*I shall spend the holidays working.*
Onde é que procurarás?	*Where will you search?*
Irá à casa deles para saber a verdade.	*He will go to their house to find out the truth.*
Partiremos às seis.	*We'll leave at six.*
Encontrareis o Senhor em todas partes.	*You will find the Lord everywhere.*
Vocês não comerão mais?	*Will you not eat more?*
Direi tudo o que sei.	*I'll say everything I know.*
Ela fará o possível.	*She will do what she can.*
Traremos o cão também.	*We shall bring the dog as well.*

The future tense can also express conjecture with reference to a present situation.

Onde estarão as crianças?	*Where can the children be?*
Estarão na escola – são dez horas.	*They'll probably be at school – it's ten o'clock.*

Vai ser muito difícil. Será?	*It's going to be very difficult. Will it?* (Do you think so? / Are you sure?)

Often, the future is rendered simply by using the verb **ir** (*to go*), plus an infinitive, just as it is in English.

Vou falar com ele amanhã.	*I'm going to talk to him tomorrow.*
Vamos passear pelo parque hoje.	*We're going to have a stroll through the park today.*
Você vai ajudar?	*Are you going to help?*

Speakers of Portuguese simplify matters even more, by using the present tense to convey the future, especially when they are speaking.

Onde vocês vão amanhã?	*Where are you going tomorrow?*
Compro um jornal no domingo.	*I'll buy a paper on Sunday.*
Vejo o meu amigo mais tarde.	*I'll see my friend later.*

Don't forget the position of object pronouns with the future tense (Unit 17). Look at this example from a horoscope:

Sentir-se-á dinâmica e mais competitiva.	*You will feel* (yourself) *dynamic and more competitive.*

Exercises

A Here is an itinerary for a week's holiday in Brazil. Say what you will do in the 'we' form on each day, using the future tense.

BRASIL – A MARAVILHA!

Sáb. – Chegar ao hotel 15:30	1
Dom. – Visita do local de ônibus [EP = autocarro]	2
Seg. – Excursão ao Rio de Janeiro	3
Ter. – Dia livre para compras	4
Qua. – Jantar especial em restaurante Gaúcho	5
Qui. – Explorar a costa	6
Sex. – Espétaculo [EP = espectáculo] de samba	7
Sáb. – Partir às 09:30	8

B Translate into Portuguese

1 We shall buy a new house.
2 Where is Sara? Could she be ill?
3 Tomorrow we're going to wash the car.
4 The plane arrives (will arrive) at 8.15.
5 I shall stay with them a week.
6 He will never go to the theatre.
7 Are you (**você**) going to visit John next week?
8 This afternoon they're going to work in the garden.
9 He's going to Bahia. Do you think it'll be hot?
10 We'll finish the journey in Lisbon.

Grammar in context

The following extract from a leaflet advertising visits round a
Port Wine Lodge in Oporto names a number of things the
visitor will experience. What are they?

1 Ser-lhe-á oferecida.....
2 Terá oportunidade...
3 Poderá ver...
4 Provará...

**Convidamo-lo a visitar as Caves de Vinho do Porto Graham's
em Vila Nova de Gaia. À sua chegada, ser-lhe-á oferecida uma
visita detalhada às caves do Vinho do Porto e terá
oportunidade de admirar centenas de cascos onde o Vinho do
Porto envelhece lentamente. Poderá ver um vídeo que mostra
as origens e a sublime arte da produção e do lotamento dos
Vinhos do Porto Graham's. No final da visita provará os
excelentes Portos enquanto aprecia a magnífica vista sobre a
parte antiga da cidade do Porto. Aguardamos a sua visita.**

29

conditional tense

In this unit you will learn
- the formation and use of the
  conditional tense in
  Portuguese

Grammar in focus

The conditional tense is used to express a variety of situations, but mainly those which are dependent on a previously stated, or understood, condition. In English we often express the conditional with *would* and *should*. As for the future, there is just one set of verb endings, added on to the infinitive of any verb, and the three irregulars met in the previous unit also have spelling changes here. Let us look at the formation and then the uses for this tense.

	all verbs
eu	+ ia
tu	+ ias
ele / ela / você	+ ia
nós	+ íamos
vós	+ íeis
eles / elas / vocês	+ iam

The three irregulars are: **dizer** (*to say*), which becomes **dir** + endings, **fazer** (*to do / make*), which becomes **far** + endings, and **trazer** (*to bring*), becoming **trar** + endings.

Don't forget the position of the object pronouns with the conditional. See Unit 17.

Uses

• To speak about actions which are not likely to come about, owing to a condition being imposed on the situation.

Gostaríamos de visitar o Japão, mas não temos tempo.	*We would like to visit Japan, but we don't have time.*
Iria com vocês, mas infelizmente o meu carro avariou-se.	*I would go with you but unfortunately my car has broken down.*

• To express wants and wishes.

Gostaria de comer fora.	*I would like to eat out.*
Dariam tudo para morar lá.	*They would give everything / anything to live there.*

- To express polite requests (alternative to the use of the imperfect seen in Unit 26).

Poderia abrir a janela para mim, por favor?	*Would (could) you open the window for me, please?*
Daria o livro ao teu irmão?	*Would you give the book to your brother?*

- To make a suggestion.

Não seria melhor descansar um pouco?	*Wouldn't it be better to rest a little?*
Deveríamos comprar mais leite.	*We should (ought to) buy more milk.*

In all the above examples, the conditional may be, and often is, substituted by the imperfect tense, especially in the spoken language (though not in BP).

Gostava de comer em casa.	*I would like to eat at home.*
Não era melhor tomar uma aspirina?	*Wouldn't it be better to take an aspirin?*

The conditional tense is also used, mainly in the written language, and especially in the media, to express an action which would come about after the main past action already described.

Começou como técnico de computadores há cinco anos e dentro de quatro anos seria chefe de uma cadeia de lojas, e milionário também.	*He started as a computer technician five years ago, and within four years was to become (would become) boss of a chain of shops, and also a millionaire.*

Exercises

A Complete the sentences by choosing a verb from those given to form conditionals.

1 .... de ir ao cinema, mas tenho muito trabalho.
   gostaria   gostei   gostariam
2 Com mil libras, ele .... um carro.
   compraríamos   compraria   compro
3 .... tudo para te ajudar.
   daríamos   darias   demos
4 Quem .... ajudar?
   poderias   poderia   pôde

5 Vocês não .... fazer isso.
deveríamos   devíamos   deveriam
6 Vi um filme tão bom que o .... outra vez.
veria   venderia   viria

B Change the verbs in **bold** from the imperfect tense used colloquially in place of the conditional, into the conditional itself.

1 Eles **iam** à festa, mas já não têm tempo.
2 Não **podíamos** ficar tanto tempo.
3 O que **gostavas** de comer?
4 **Ajudava** se podia.
5 Ela **adorava** passar as férias no Brasil.
6 Eu não me **importava** de estudar mais.
7 Quanto **davam** para ver Roberto Carlos?
8 Acho que **devias** reclamar sobre o preço.
9 **Era** mais fácil tentar de manhã.
10 Sem carro eu não **ia.**

Grammar in context

Read these thoughts from a potential winner of the jackpot in TotoLoto in Portugal, and decide what she says she would do if she won.

Se eu ganhasse um grande prémio... (*If I won a huge prize...*)

Compraria um novo carro Mercedes.
Visitaria a minha irmã nos Estados Unidos.
Iríamos à Costa Verde para umas férias na praia.
Mudaria de emprego – gostaria de ter a minha própria (*own*) loja.
Mudaríamos de casa – mais perto dos meus pais.
Ao meu filho mais velho daria o dinheiro para comprar uma motocicleta.
À minha filha eu mandaria para a Universidade na França.
E claro, doaria (*donate*) alguma coisa à nossa igreja.

30

ter and haver

In this unit you will learn
- how to form and use the verbs ter and haver in various tenses and phrases

Grammar in focus

Both of these verbs express *to have* in Portuguese, but they are used in different circumstances, and can alter their meanings accordingly. **Ter** is the more regularly used verb, while **haver** has a more limited function.

The two verbs are given in full in the present tense in this unit; for their formation in other tenses, see Unit 37 and the verb tables on pages 263–71.

Ter

eu	tenho	*I have*
tu	tens	*you have*
ele / ela / você	tem	*he / she / it / has / you have*
nós	temos	*we have*
vós	tendes	*you have*
eles / elas / vocês	têm	*they / you* (pl.) *have*

Ter is used in the following situations:

• To express possession.

A Maria tem um carro verde. *Maria has a green car.*
Eu tinha uma boneca bonita. *I used to have a pretty doll.*

• With ages.

Quantos anos tem o João?   *How old is João?   He's eight.*
   Tem oito.
Tínhamos seis anos quando   *We were six when we moved*
   mudámos de casa.   *house.*

• To describe a problem or illness.

O que é que tens? Pareces   *What's wrong? You seem*
   agitada.   *nervous.*
Tenho dores de cabeça.   *My head hurts.*

• Other common usages include:

ter: medo (*to be afraid*), calor (*to be hot*), frio (*to be cold*), pressa (*to be in a hurry*), fome (*to be hungry*), sorte (*to be lucky*), sede (*to be thirsty*), sono (*to be tired / sleepy*).

Ter de, ter que

Ter is also used in these interchangeable expressions, to denote necessity or obligation. See Unit 35.

Não temos pão; vamos ter
   de ir à padaria.
O Paulo teve que voltar para
   casa.

*We have no bread; we'll have
   to go to the baker's.*
Paulo had to return home.

Ter in compound tenses

Ter is used as the auxiliary (lead) verb in the compound tenses (see Units 32 and 33).

Esta semana, a Ana tem
   trabalhado muito.
Tinham chegado depois da
   festa.

*This week Ana has been
   working a lot.*
*They had arrived after the
   party.*

Haver

eu	hei
tu	hás
ele / ela / você	há
nós	havemos
vós	haveis
eles / elas / vocês	hão

Haver is used in the following situations, primarily in the third person singular:

- To mean *there is, there are, there was* etc.*

   Há um banco na rua
      25 de Abril.
   Havia muito para visitar.

   *There is a bank on 25 de Abril
      Street.*
   There was a lot to visit.

- To denote an event or occurrence.*

   No sábado houve uma
      partida de futebol na
      televisão.
   Houve um acidente na praça.

   *On Saturday there was a
      football match on the
      television.*
   *There was an accident in the
      square.*

   Que barulho! O que é que
      há?

   *What a noise! What's going
      on?*

- To describe temporary weather conditions.*

   Não havia muito sol durante
      as férias.
   Há vento no norte.

   *There wasn't much sun during
      the holidays.*
   It's windy in the north.

*Brazilians have tended more and more to use ter in place of haver in this case:
Tem um banco, Tinha muito sol etc.

Expressions of time

Haver is used to denote the passage of time (**haver** + unit of time). It is used in the present tense to denote *has / have*, and in the imperfect to denote *had*, with the corresponding verb in the sentence in the same tense. It also means *ago*.

Estamos a esperar há muito tempo.	*We have been waiting for a long time.*
Eles chegaram há uma hora.	*They arrived an hour ago.*
Havia muitos anos que eu não via o José.	*I had not seen José for many years.*
Tinha visitado o pai havia duas semanas.	*He had visited his father two weeks previously.*

Haver de + infinitive

Although this construction is not widely used, it denotes strong intention to do something. The word **de** is joined with a hyphen to the verb forms **hei, hás, há** and **hão** in European Portuguese, but not in Brazil. See also Unit 35.

Qualquer dia eu hei-de nadar bem, faço tanto esforço na piscina.	*One day I will swim well, I put in so much effort at the pool.*
Não tinham dinheiro, então o que haviam de fazer?	*They had no money, so what on earth could they do?*
Havemos de ganhar na lotaria esta semana.	*We've got to win the lottery this week.*

Haver in compound tenses

The use of **haver** as an auxiliary verb is quite outdated, and usually reserved for highly literary styles of writing, apart from in Brazil, where the pluperfect (*had done*) is often expressed by **havia** + past participle, instead of **tinha**, more so in the written language.

O Conde de Milfontes haverá chegado a Braga antes do Rei.	*The Count of Milfontes will have arrived in Braga before the King.*
Eles haviam ido à praia.	*They had gone to the beach.*

Haver through the tenses

Here is a brief overview of the basic form of **haver** in different tenses. See also Unit 37.

há	*there is / are*
havia	*there was / were*
houve	*there was / were / has / have been*
tinha havido	*there had been*

tem havido   *there has been*
haverá   *there will be*
haveria   *there would be*

Exercises

A Decide which of the two verb forms is correct in each example. In some cases both are possible.

1 Eu (tenho / hei-de) uma casa bonita.
2 Tu (tens / hás-de) falar português bem um dia.
3 Ele (tem / há-de) vinte anos.
4 Ela está cá (tem / há) muito tempo.
5 Você (tem / há-de) sono?
6 (Tinha / Havia) muita chuva em Junho.
7 O que (têm / hão) as senhoras? Estão muito tristes.
8 (Teve / Houve) um concerto no palácio.
9 (Temos que / Havemos de) visitar a minha amiga no hospital.
10 (Tem / Há) muitas lojas no centro.

B Have a look at this text describing the Happy Ostrich Farm and its facilities. How much of it can you understand, with the help of the vocabulary box? Answer the questions below it.

A Quinta da Avestruz Alegre – the Happy Ostrich Farm

Localizada em Tavira, a quinta promete uma visita de momentos animados. Tem como atracção principal as avestruzes, mas não é tudo! Também há cangurus, esquilos, muitas espécies de coelhos, e outros animais incríveis neste parque divertido. Para os adultos, há um bar, onde podem relaxar enquanto a criançada brinca nos túneis de madeira, e no castelo insuflável. A Aldeia Exótica tem exposições e diversões para toda a família.

A Quinta oferece horas de divertimento.

Horário: De Segunda a Sexta: 09h00 às 20h00 / Sábado: 10h00 às 18h00

Não existe nada igual no Algarve!

a quinta promete	*the farm promises*
não é tudo!	*that's not all!*
cangurus,	*kangaroos,*
esquilos, coelhos	*squirrels, rabbits*
divertido	*fun, entertaining*
a criançada	*the youngsters*
	(singular in Portuguese)
brinca	*play(s)*
túneis de madeira	*wooden tunnels*
castelo insuflável	*bouncy castle*
a Aldeia Exótica	*the Exotic Village*
exposicões, diversões	*displays, activities*
nada igual	*nothing like it*

1 True or false?

a The farm is found in Tavira.
b You cannot find squirrels at the farm.
c Children can play on a bouncy castle.
d The 'Exotic Village' has activities for all the family.
e The attraction opens at 9 a.m. on Saturdays.

2 How many examples of **ter** and **haver** can you find?

Grammar in context

The following tongue-twister (**trava-línguas**) was sent into a Portuguese magazine by youngster Rute Luz. Can you work out what it means? And can you say it? A great party-piece!

O que é que há cá?
É o eco que há cá.
Há cá eco?
Há cá eco, há.

31

participles

In this unit you will learn
- about the present and past
  participles and their uses

Grammar in focus

Participles are parts of verbs, sometimes used on their own, but often in conjunction with other verbs. There is a present and a past participle.

Present participle

This form of the verb corresponds to English *-ing*. It is also known as the gerund. It is formed by adding these endings to the **stem** of any verb:

-ar verbs	*-er* verbs	*-ir* verbs
+ ando	+ endo	+ indo

These endings are the same for whichever person is doing the action.

falando *speaking* comendo *eating* partindo *leaving / breaking*

The gerund is used:

- To substitute a (second or third) main verb in a sentence which conveys a follow-on action from a previous verb. Instead of having a list of completed actions, one of them may become a gerund.

  Comeram um jantar
    delicioso e ouviram boa
    música do grupo.
  *They ate a delicious dinner
    and heard good music from
    the group.*

  Comeram um jantar
    delicioso, ouvindo boa
    música do grupo.
  *They ate a delicious dinner,
    hearing good music from
    the group.*

- To substitute time expressions such as **quando** (*when*) + main verb, or **ao** (*on*) + infinitive.

  Quando cheguei a casa,
    acendi as luzes.
  *When I arrived home I
    switched on the lights.*

  Chegando a casa...
  Arriving home...

  Ao ver o comboio [BP trem]
    parar, ele saiu do carro.
  *On seeing the train stop, he
    got out of his car.*

  Vendo o comboio parar...
  Seeing the train stop...

- To indicate how something is happening – as a response to the question **Como?**

  Ela olhou as flores com um
    sorriso.
  *She looked at the flowers with
    a smile.*

  Ela olhou as flores sorrindo.
  *She looked at the flowers,
    smiling.*

Como é que partiu a perna? *How did he break his leg?*
   Esquiando.   *Ski-ing.*

* Brazilians use the gerund form in continuous tenses, whereas in Portugal the construction **estar + a +** infinitive is used (see Unit 34).

Ela estava dormindo quando   *She was sleeping when they*
   chegaram.   *arrived.*

Ir + gerund

The verb **ir** (*to go*) is used with the gerund to express a situation where someone is 'getting on with' or 'carrying on with' an action.

Vão comendo, que eu já vou.   *You carry on eating, I'll be*
                                 there soon.

Enquanto a Manuela foi ao   *Whilst Manuela went to the*
   mercado, a Laura foi   *market, Laura carried on*
   arrumando a casa.   *tidying the house.*

Vai preparando o almoço, que   *You get on with preparing*
   eu volto à meio-dia.   *lunch, as I'll be back at*
                                 midday.

Past participle

The past participle is the part of the verb that is used in 'compound tenses' – those made up of more than one verb (*have* [English] / **ter** [Portuguese] + the action verb), such as *I had talked* / **tinha falado**. Past participles are also used as adjectives, with the verbs *to be* (**ser** and **estar**), and with **ficar** (*to stay, remain, become*), **andar** (*to walk, frequent, act in a certain way* – colloquially), **ir** (*to go*) and **vir** (*to come*). They form part of the passive voice (see Unit 39).

The past participle for regular verbs is formed by adding these endings to the stem of any verb:

-ar verbs	*-er* verbs	*-ir* verbs
+ ado	+ ido	+ ido

The endings are the same for any person. However, when the participles are used as adjectives, their endings change according to the normal rules of agreement. (Look back at Unit 3.)

Eu tinha arrumado o meu   *I had tidied my room.*
   quarto.

O Paulo não tem comido   *Paulo hasn't eaten a lot this*
   muito esta semana.   *week.*

Nós teremos partido antes da tua chegada.	*We will have left before your arrival.*
A janela foi partida pela bola.	*The window was broken by the ball.*
O leão estava adormecido.	*The lion was asleep.*
Ela ficou supreendida.	*She was (became) surprised.*

Irregular verbs – irregular past participles

As you might expect, some verbs, both regular and irregular, have irregular past participles, which you should learn along with the verb itself. You will soon start to recognize them if you are reading Portuguese papers and magazines. Here are the main ones – you can also refer to the verb tables on pages 263–71.

dizer *to say*	dito *said*
abrir *to open*	aberto *opened*
escrever *to write*	escrito *written*
fazer *to do / make*	feito *done / made*
ganhar *to win*	ganho *won*
gastar *to spend*	gasto *spent*
pagar *to pay*	pago *paid*
pôr *to put*	posto *put*
ver *to see*	visto *seen*
vir *to come*	vindo *come* (same as the gerund)

Double participles

There are also a number of verbs in Portuguese that have two past participles. The regular one, formed as explained above, is used in the compound tenses, and does not change its ending, but the irregular forms are the ones used with the verbs **ser** and **estar, ficar, andar, ir** and **vir,** and will change their endings as adjectives. The following verbs act in this way.

		Regular (used in tenses)	Irregular (with *ser, estar* etc.)
aceitar	*to accept*	aceitado	aceito (BP) *or* aceite
acender	*to light*	acendido	aceso
entregar	*to hand over*	entregado	entregue
enxugar	*to dry*	enxugado	enxuto
expulsar	*to expel*	expulsado	expulso
limpar	*to clean*	limpado	limpo
matar	*to kill*	matado	morto
omitir	*to omit*	omitido	omisso
prender	*to fasten / arrest*	prendido	preso

		Regular (used in tenses)	Irregular (with *ser*, *estar* etc.)
romper	*to tear*	rompido	roto
salvar	*to save*	salvado	salvo
secar	*to dry*	secado	seco
soltar	*to let loose*	soltado	solto
suspender	*to suspend*	suspendido	suspenso

Ele tinha limpado o carro.	*He had cleaned the car.*
O carro está limpo.	*The car is clean* (cleaned).
Tinham expulsado o coronel.	*They had expelled the Colonel.*
Não tenho pago as contas.	*I've not been paying* (paid) *the bills.*
Todas as portas estavam abertas.	*All the doors were open.*
O nosso cartão não foi aceite.	*Our card was not accepted.*

Exercises

A Choose the correct participle from the box to describe what has happened in each picture. Be sure to check which auxiliary verb is being used in each case, as that may affect the participle you require.

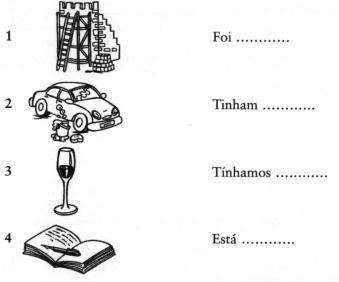

1   Foi ....

2   Tinham ....

3   Tínhamos ....

4   Está ....

5 Ficou ....

6 Está ....

7 Foi ....

8 Andava ....

aberto	limpado / limpo	furado
bebido	pintado	rompido / roto
construído	pago	prendido / preso	escrito

B Complete the following table with infinitives, and present and past participles, and their meanings in English.

beber	bebendo	*drinking*	bebido	*drunk*
lavar	....	*washing*	....	*washed*
....	rindo	*laughing*	....	....
....	vindo	....	....	*come*
pagar	....	....	....	*paid*
....	....	*singing*	cantado	....
receber	recebendo	....	....	....
abrir	....	....	....	*open*
....	vendo	*seeing*	....	....

Grammar in context

1 At the Solar Tropical restaurant in Brazil, each night a type of show presents the best exponents of **Capoeira** (a Brazilian dance form). What details are given about the folklore?

2 At the Apolo 71 pastelaria, which three past participles mean: *processed, included, indicated*?

A melhor cozinha baiana e os frutos do mar no mais tradicional Solar da Baía de Todos os Santos. Todas as noites o mais autêntico show folclórico apresentando os melhores mestres da Capoeira de Angola e Regional.

SOLAR TROPICAL

Restaurante

Av. do Contorno, 08 – Cidade Baixa
Reservas: (071) 321–5551

APOLO 71 PASTELARIA
Av. da Cruz, Silves
Factura/Recibo: 035798726

Produto	Qnt.	Sub T.	IVA
Pastel	1	1,20 €	12
Bolo	1	1,75 €	12
Café	1	1,00 €	12
Chá	1	1,25 €	12
TOTAL:	Euros	5,20 €	

Documento processado por Computador.
IVA incluído a taxa indicada.

MESA: 3

Obrigado. Volte sempre!

32

compound tenses – present perfect

In this unit you will learn
- the formation of compound tenses: the present perfect and its uses

Grammar in focus

The 'perfect' tenses in Portuguese are those made up of more than one verb, and so are known as compound tenses. They are formed by placing the verb **ter**, *to have* (known as an 'auxiliary' verb and conjugated according to person and time), before the past participle of any verb conveying the action.

The present perfect is formed with the present tense of the verb **ter** and a past participle of the main verb. It conveys an action which has started in the past and has been taking place with some modicum of regularity, with a connection up to the present time. At this point the action may, or may not, have stopped.

falar - *I have spoken, been speaking*, etc.

tenho	falado	temos	falado
tens	falado	tendes	falado
tem	falado	têm	falado

```
                    PAST              NOW
_____X_____→_I_____>
```

Não temos falado muito esta semana.	*We have not spoken much this week.*
Ela tem trabalhado tanto que já não se sente bem.	*She has (been working) worked so much that now she doesn't feel well.*
Tens visto o Miguel ultimamente?	*Have you seen Miguel recently?*
Tenho comprado muitos livros desde o começo do curso.	*I've bought a lot of books since the beginning of the course.*
O preço das bananas tem aumentado nestes últimos anos.	*The price of bananas has gone up (been going up) in the last few years.*

Position of pronouns with perfect tenses

In perfect tenses, pronouns become connected to the auxiliary verb (**ter**), and not the main verb, which is now a past participle and not 'strong' enough to hold a pronoun. The normal rules of position still apply.

Ultimamente tenho-me levantado cedo.	*Recently I have been getting up / got up early.*
O meu irmão não se tem levantado tão cedo.	*My brother has not been getting up / got up so early.*

Exercises

A Use the words indicated and put the verbs into the correct form to make complete sentences in the present perfect.

1 Tu / ver / as partidas de futebol?
2 Eu / ter / muito trabalho.
3 Fazer / muito sol este ano.
4 Eu / não falar / italiano ultimamente.
5 Ele / não vir / ao colégio muito desde Janeiro.
6 Nós / perder / muito dinheiro no casino.
7 Eles / ir / às aulas desde que começaram o curso.
8 A minha mulher / trabalhar / demais.
9 Ela / não descansar / desde o ano passado.
10 Elas / estar / doentes.

B Match the questions to an appropriate response.

1 O que tens feito esta semana?
2 Porque não têm vindo às aulas?
3 Como se tem sentido estes dias?
4 Como está o tempo aí?
5 Como vão as vendas?
6 O que é que eles têm andado a fazer?
7 Tens comido bem?
8 Porque está cansada?

a Bem – ultimamente temos vendido muito.
b Tenho-me sentido muito melhor.
c Porque não tenho dormido bem esta semana.
d Têm estudado e não têm saído.
e Só tenho trabalhado.
f Não, não tenho tido apetite.
g Porque têm estado doentes.
h Este mês só tem chovido.

Grammar in context

In a magazine interview, Portuguese entertainer Quim Barreiros talks about finally getting time to take a holiday. What has he been doing in recent years?

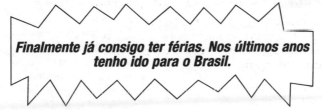

Finalmente já consigo ter férias. Nos últimos anos tenho ido para o Brasil.

33

other compound tenses

In this unit you will learn
- how to form and use other compound tenses: the pluperfect, future perfect and conditional tenses

Grammar in focus

Pluperfect (past perfect)

The pluperfect is formed by using the imperfect tense of the verb ter with the past participle of the main verb. In Brazil, the written language is more likely to use **haver** as the auxiliary verb instead of **ter**. This tense conveys the equivalent of the English *had done* – for actions which are completed in the past before another past action takes place.

falar *I had spoken, you had spoken*, etc.

tinha	falado	tínhamos	falado
tinhas	falado	tínheis	falado
tinha	falado	tinham	falado

PAST	PAST	NOW
X	x	I >

Pluperfect

O avião já tinha partido quando eles chegaram ao aeroporto.	*The plane had already departed when they arrived at the airport.*
Eu tinha-me esforçado muito, mas não consegui fazê-lo.	*I had tried really hard, but I didn't manage to do it.*
Eles não se haviam comunicado em muitos anos.	*They had not been in touch for many years.*

There is also a non-compound tense, sometimes referred to as the 'synthetic' (or 'simple') pluperfect. It is used mainly in the written language, and formed as follows:

- Take the third person plural of the preterite of any verb, remove the ending **-ram**, and add the following set of endings: **-ra / -ras / -ra / -ramos / -reis / -ram**.

- In the first and second person plural, the preceding syllable requires an accent.

Although you will rarely use this tense, it does occur in some interesting idiomatic phrases, mostly in the first person.

Tomara eu / tomáramos nós + infinitive	*If only I / we could...*
Quem me / nos dera + infinitive	*If only I / we could...*
Pudera!	*No wonder!*

The third person plural form is very rare, as it is identical to the preterite – the compound equivalent is used instead.

Future perfect

This tense is formed with the future tense of the verb **ter** plus the past participle of the main verb. It expresses *will have done*, describing future actions taking place before or after other future actions.

Comer *I will have eaten, you will have eaten,* etc.

terei	comido	teremos	comido
terás	comido	tereis	comido
terá	comido	terão	comido

```
           NOW          FUTURE          FUTURE
_____I___>>_____X_____x_____>
```

Não teremos vendido a casa antes de viajar.	*We will not have sold the house before travelling.*
O Carlos terá chegado antes do pai.	*Carlos will have arrived before his father.*
Daqui a seis horas terei escrito tudo.	*In six hours' time I'll have written everything.*

The future perfect can also be used to express doubt over past situations or facts.

A Lia está atrasada; o que terá acontecido?	*Lia is late; what can (will) have happened?*
Terá havido muito trânsito?	*Can (will) there have been a lot of traffic?*

It is also employed frequently in the media to express conjecture over past facts and situations, and conveys the idea of *must have…* .

O ladrão terá fugido com o dinheiro num saco.	*The thief will (must) have fled with the money in a bag.* (supposedly / allegedly / apparently)

Conditional perfect

This tense is formed with the conditional of the verb **ter**, plus the past participle of the main verb. It conveys the English *would have done*, and is used in conditional, or 'If' sentences (see also Unit 45). It expresses actions in the past which have not taken place because of a condition being imposed on them, whether this is expressed or not. In the colloquial language (EP), the conditional part of **ter** can be replaced with the imperfect form.

Partir *I would have left, you would have left,* etc.

teria	partido	teríamos	partido
terias	partido	teríeis	partido
teria	partido	teriam	partido

A Sra. D. Maria Silva teria comprado a casa, mas era muito velha.	*Mrs Silva would have bought the house, but it was very old.*
Eu não teria dado tanto dinheiro, mas parecia doente.	*I would not have given so much money, but he seemed ill.*
Se não tivéssemos chegado tão tarde, tínhamos encontrado todo o mundo em casa.	*If we had not arrived so late, we would have found everyone at home.*

Like the future perfect, the conditional perfect is also used in the media to express uncertainty about actions which have taken place.

Não se sabe muito acerca dos acontecimentos, mas o homem teria ameaçado a empregada com uma pistola.	*Not much is known about what happened, but the man must have (would have) / allegedly threatened the maid with a pistol.*

Exercises

A Look at the actions that have taken place and complete the final box to link the two actions together. Then translate all three boxes. The first is done as an example.

Happened first	Happened next	
O barco partiu (**partir**)	O João chegou	O barco (já) **tinha partido** quando o João chegou.
The boat left	*João arrived*	*The boat had (already) left when João arrived.*

1

A tua filha saiu (**sair**)	Tu chegaste a casa	

2

O 'show' começou (**começar**)	Entrámos no teatro	

3 Ele pagou a conta (**pagar**)	Ela chamou o empregado	

4 Nós fomos ao centro (**ir**)	Tu telefonaste	

5 Ela fez o jantar (**fazer**)	O programa começou	

B Decide which compound tense fits in each sentence, and form the verb accordingly.

1 Eu já **ter comer** quando eles chegaram.
2 Daqui a três semanas eles **ter terminar** a escola.
3 O que **ter fazer** tu nessa situação?
4 Se não tivessem comprado o carro, **ter poder** ir de férias.
5 Onde está o Manuel? Onde **ter ir**?
6 Em cinco horas nós **ter pintar** o quarto.
7 Quando chegámos, ela ainda não **ter preparar** nada.
8 Provavelmente o roubo **ter acontecer** durante a noite.

Language watch 5

Use your knowledge of other languages to make a sensible guess at unknown words in Portuguese. In Latin-based languages, perfect or near-perfect cognates (similar words) exist across the range. Note the following examples as a starting point, and look out for more as you proceed.

Portuguese	Spanish	Italian	French	English
pão	pan	pane	pain	bread
mês	mes	mese	mois	month
mãe	madre	madre	mère	mother
novo	nuevo	nuovo	nouveau	new
noite	noche	notte	nuit	night
três	tres	tre	trois	three
cereja	cereza	ciliegia	cerise	cherry

34

continuous tenses

Grammar in focus

The continuous, or progressive, tenses express actions that are considered to be in progress, continuing, or unfinished. The continuous formation in Portugal consists of the appropriate tense of the verb **estar** (*to be*), plus **a**, plus the infinitive of the main verb. In Brazil, the formation is **estar** + gerund. (Look back at Unit 31.) The tenses correspond to English *is doing, was doing, will be doing* etc. for actions in progress

Present continuous

Falar *I am speaking, you are speaking*, etc.

	Portugal	Brazil
eu *I*	estou a falar	estou falando
tu *you*	estás a falar	estás falando
ele / ela *he / she*	está a falar	está falando
você *you*	está a falar	está falando
nós *we*	estamos a falar	estamos falando
vós *you* pl.	estais a falar	estais falando
eles / elas *they*	estão a falar	estão falando
vocês *you* pl.	estão a falar	estão falando

Com quem estás a falar?   *With whom are you talking?*
O que estão comprando?   *What are you buying?*
Ela está a chorar.   *She is crying.*
Não estamos fazendo nada.   *We are not doing anything.*
Estou a pôr a mesa.   *I am laying / setting the table.*

Imperfect continuous

Comer *I was speaking, you were speaking*, etc.

	Portugal	Brazil
eu *I*	estava a comer	estava comendo
tu *you*	estavas a comer	estavas comendo
ele / ela *he / she*	estava a comer	estava comendo
você *you*	estava a comer	estava comendo
nós *we*	estávamos a comer	estávamos comendo
vós *you* pl.	estáveis a comer	estáveis comendo
eles / elas *they*	estavam a comer	estavam comendo
vocês *you* pl.	estavam a comer	estavam comendo

Eu estava a comer quando eles chegaram.	*I was eating when they arrived.*
O que estavas lendo?	*What were you reading?*
Não estávamos a correr.	*We were not running.*
Ela estava dando bilhetes a todos.	*She was giving tickets to everyone.*
Você não estava a dizer a verdade.	*You were not telling the truth.*

Future continuous

Partir *I will be leaving, you will be leaving,* etc.

	Portugal	Brazil
eu *I*	estarei a partir	estarei partindo
tu *you*	estarás a partir	estarás partindo
ele / ela *he / she*	estará a partir	estará partindo
você *you*	estará a partir	estará partindo
nós *we*	estaremos a partir	estaremos partindo
vós *you* pl.	estareis a partir	estareis partindo
eles / elas *they*	estarão a partir	estarão partindo
vocês *you* pl.	estarão a partir	estarão partindo

Estarei a partir amanhã.	*I'll be leaving tomorrow.*
O Nuno estará abrindo a nova loja.	*Nuno will be opening the new shop.*
Estaremos a assistir à peça.	*We will be watching the play.*
O que estarão fazendo?	*What can (will) they be doing?*
Provavelmente estarão brincando.	*They'll probably be playing.*

Theoretically, the progressive form can be made with any of the tenses, but in practice it is often substituted by other, simple tenses, such as the present. However, here is a summary of the formations of other tenses for **falar**.

Summary of continuous tenses

Present	estou a falar / falando	*I am speaking*
Imperfect	estava a falar / falando	*I was speaking*
Preterite	estive a falar / falando	*I was / have been speaking*
Synthetic pluperfect	estivera a falar / falando	*I had been speaking*
Future	estarei a falar / falando	*I will be speaking*

Conditional	estaria a falar / falando	*I would be speaking*
Present perfect	tenho estado a falar / falando	*I have been speaking*
Pluperfect	tinha estado a falar / falando	*I had been speaking*
Future perfect	terei estado a falar / falando	*I will have been speaking*
Conditional perfect	teria estado a falar / falando	*I would have been speaking*

Keep in mind that, in practice, particularly in spoken language, very few of these forms are used. Other auxiliary verbs used to express a progressive action are **continuar** (*to continue*), **seguir** (*to follow; to go on*), **ir** (*to go*), **andar** (*to go about*) and **ficar** (*to stay, remain; to continue*).

Ele continua a fazer erros.	*He continues to make mistakes.*
Seguimos dançando até à meia-noite.	*We carried on dancing until midnight.*
Elas vão passeando pelo parque.	*They go strolling through the park.*
Vai comendo.	*Carry on eating.*
Eu ando a trabalhar muito.	*I'm working a lot.*
Ficámos bebendo a noite inteira.	*We kept on drinking all night long.*

Exercises

A Describe what is happening in each picture, using the Present continuous (European or Brazilian forms).

1  Eu   correr

2  Eles comer

3  Você pagar

4 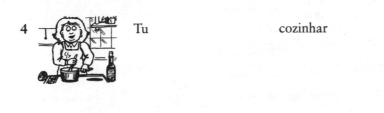 Tu cozinhar

5 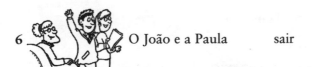 Nós nadar

6 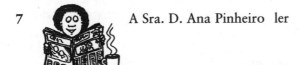 O João e a Paula sair

7 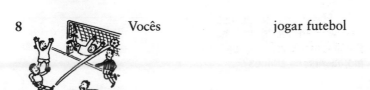 A Sra. D. Ana Pinheiro ler

8 Vocês jogar futebol

B Look at the imaginary diary of Carmen's pet cat Pitufa. Then complete the sentences to show what Pitufa was doing at certain points during the day.

Quarta-feira 🐈
08:30 – comer
10:00 – sair para passeio
11:45 – dormir
13:30 – beber água
15:15 – dormir
17:40 – jantar
18:00 – passear na rua
20:10 – ver programa de natureza na TV
22:15 – dormir

O que é que a Pitufa estava a fazer...

1 às onze e 45
2 às seis menos vinte
3 às oito e dez da noite
4 à uma e meia
5 às seis da tarde
6 às oito e meia da manhã?

Grammar in context

Read this letter, sent to a letters page of the Brazilian magazine *Cláudia*. The writer wants to know about the etiquette of greeting people on arriving at a party. What is she in doubt about (**na dúvida**)?

Quem cumprimentar primeiro numa festa?

Quando vou a uma festa, fico na dúvida: ao me dirigir ao anfitrião, devo ir parando para cumprimentar os amigos?

Jas, Rio.

anfitrião *host*

35

modal auxiliaries - must / ought / should / could

In this unit you will learn
- how to express obligation, necessity and possibility in Portuguese (*must, ought, should, could*)

Grammar in focus

In Portuguese there are different ways to convey the idea of 'having to' do something, depending on how strong the conviction is. The verbs **dever**, **ter de / que**, **precisar de** and **haver de** are all used. To translate situations involving the word *could* = *be able*, the verb **poder** is used. Different tenses can be used for a variety of situations. The verbs are known here as modal 'auxiliaries' because they are all used in combination with a main verb in the infinitive.

Dever

Can convey moral obligation – what you must, must not, should or should not do – and is often used in giving advice to people. It also expresses probability, in ideas of supposition.

Um atleta deve comer bem.	*An athlete must eat well.*
Não deverias fumar tanto.	*You shouldn't (ought not to) smoke so much.*
Onde está a Mónica? Deve ter saído.	*Where is Monica? She must have gone out.*
Deveriam ter comprado os bilhetes antes.	*They should have (ought to have) bought the tickets earlier.*

Ter de / que

Conveys a strong necessity to carry out an action, sometimes involving obligation from outside forces. It is used very much in everyday Portuguese.

Tenho de comprar pão hoje.	*I have to buy bread today.*
Para ser médico tem que estudar muito.	*To be a doctor you have to study hard.*
A sua filha tem de tomar o xarope de cinco em cinco horas.	*Your daughter must (has to) take the cough syrup every five hours.*
Tinham que devolver o dinheiro.	*They had to give the money back.*

Precisar de

Conveys general need, or necessity.

Precisamos de vender o carro porque não temos mais dinheiro.	*We need to sell the car because we have no money left.*
Vou precisar de cinco selos.	*I'm going to need five stamps.*
Precisas de alguma coisa?	*Do you need anything?*
Ela precisava de ajuda.	*She needed help.*

Haver de (see Unit 30)

Conveys a strong intention or conviction in respect of future action or situations. It can translate into English in a variety of ways, such as: *really have to*, *got to* and *really will*.

Havemos de ganhar esta semana.	*We've got to win this week.*
Qualquer dia, ele há-de [BP = há de] ser rico.	*One day he really will be rich.*
Hei-de [BP = hei de] encontrar o meu 'Príncipe Encantado'.	*I will find my Prince Charming.*

Poder

Conveys possibility and opportunity to do things, in the negative says what you are not allowed to do, and is also used to ask and give permission. It translates in different tenses as *can* and *could*. Remember its basic meaning is *to be able to*, and that it is followed by verbs in the infinitive, even though the English might not necessarily have one.

Não podem escrever mais hoje.	*They cannot write any more today.*
Não podemos fumar aqui dentro.	*We cannot smoke here inside.*
Posso começar? Claro que pode.	*May (can) I begin? Of course you can.*
Poderia ter feito mais para ajudar.	*She could have done more to help.*
Não podias ver?	*Couldn't you see?*

Exercises

A Match up the English statements with an appropriate response in Portuguese.

1 I wonder where Paul can be?
2 I had to wear a plaster cast for six weeks.
3 Why are they all wearing hats and scarves?
4 Ellie's complaining about her exam results.
5 Jack didn't get to the station on time.
6 We didn't get a holiday this year.
7 All those lovely cakes have been sold.
8 Why don't I ever win the lottery?
9 Are you coming to the party?
10 They never have any money these days.

a Podia ter-se levantado mais cedo.
b Não, temos de trabalhar.
c Já deve / deveria ter partido.
d Pois, tinham que comprar um novo carro.
e Deve estar frio lá fora.
f Devias / deverias ter comprado antes.
g Podiam tirar férias no ano que vem.
h Deve / deveria ter sido muito difícil para você.
i Hás-de ganhar qualquer dia.
j Podia ter estudado mais.

B Look at this list of safety instructions for what to do if you hear the fire-alarm go off in your hotel. Choose the correct verb to complete each instruction.

Ao ouvir o sinal de alarme

1 .... o quarto, e **2** .... a porta, adoptando o seu plano de fuga.
3 .... às saídas pelos caminhos de emergência.
4 .... o elevador.
5 .... junto à parede com calma, ordem e rapidez.
6 .... as orientações do pessoal do estabelecimento.

a deveria fechar
b deveria seguir
c deveria dirigir-se
d deve sempre cumprir
e deveria abandonar
f nunca deveria utilizar

Grammar in context

The following consumer advice on what you need to know as a tourist in Portugal includes guidance for eating out.

CONSUMIDOR
TURISTA

RESTAURANTES, SNACK-BARES, CAFÉS, BARES, HOTÉIS, PENSÕES, PARQUES DE CAMPISMO, AGÊNCIAS DE VIAGENS...

O QUE DEVE SABER

■ Nos restaurantes devem constar da ementa o preço e a composição do 'couvert' (manteiga, queijo fresco, azeitonas, pão torrado, etc.). Este só pode ser cobrado se for consumido ou inutilizado.

■ A lista do dia deve estar obrigatoriamente escrita em língua portuguesa.

1 What must be set out on the menu (**ementa**)? It can only be charged (**cobrado**) when?
2 What is the requirement for the menu of the day (**a lista do dia**)?

36

commands (imperatives)

In this unit you will learn
- how to tell people to do or not to do things: the **tu**, **vós**, **você** and **vocês** forms

Grammar in focus

Commands, although the word suggests something rather dominating, are really just the way you tell people to do, or not to do things. They can be as everyday as saying 'go and wash your hands'. You can 'command' a single person, or many people. The verb of the action you wish to happen or not happen will change its endings according to whether you are commanding someone in the **tu** form, the old **vós** form, or the **você** and **vocês** forms (and their polite equivalents). Strictly speaking, commands should have an exclamation mark at the end of the sentence, but in English too this does not always appear these days.

Affirmative commands

The *tu* form

The command form for **tu** (used with friends, family, young children and people of similar social rank) is exactly the same verb form as the third person singular of the present indicative.

falar	*to speak*	fala (third person singular)	Fala!	*Speak!*
comer	*to eat*	come (third person)	Come!	*Eat!*
partir	*to leave*	parte (third person)	Parte!	*Leave!*

Fala mais baixo!	*Speak more quietly!*
Come tudo!	*Eat it all up!*
Abre a porta para o senhor!	*Open the door for the gentleman!*

The same system applies to irregular verbs: take the third person singular of the present tense. This means you need to learn those fiddly irregular verbs!

Vai por aqui.	*Go along here.*
Faz o trabalho.	*Do the work.*

Note that the **tu** command of **ser** is **sê**.

The *vós* form

The archaic **vós** form is still used in church services, political speeches, and by older people in remote areas. The command form for **vós** is also based on the present indicative. The final **s** is simply removed from the second person plural (**vós**) form of the verb.

cantar	*to sing*	cantais (second person plural)	Cantai!	*Sing!*
receber	*to receive*	recebeis (second person)	Recebei!	*Receive!*
resistir	*to resist*	resistis (second person)	Resisti!	*Resist!*
ir	*to go*	ides (second person)	Ide!	*Go!*

Cantai ao Senhor.	*Sing unto the Lord.*
Bebei e comei, porque hoje é festa.	*Drink and eat, for today is a party.*
Dormi, filhos.	*Sleep, (my) children.*
Vinde, pastores...	*Come, shepherds* (first line of 'O come, all ye faithful')

The *você* form, or 'polite' commands

To command in the **você** (or third person polite) form (used with strangers, older people, and those of higher social rank; used exclusively in most of Brazil) the verb goes into what is known as the 'present subjunctive', which is another set of endings (see Units 40–4). The full subjunctive formations are given in Unit 40, but basically, -**ar** verbs take an -**er** ending, and -**er** and -**ir** verbs assume an -**ar** ending, so there is a cross-over of the usual 3rd person -**a** / -**e** endings. However, the stem for the endings is actually taken from the first person singular (*I*), so that irregular verbs do have an irregular form – check in Unit 37 and the verb tables on pages 263–71. You need to watch out for verbs which may only have an irregular spelling in the first person singular, as that spelling change carries forward throughout the subjunctive.

comprar	*to buy*	compra (third person)	→ Compre!	*Buy!*
escrever	*to write*	escreve (third person)	→ Escreva!	*Write!*
insistir	*to insist*	insiste (third person)	→ Insista!	*Insist!*
dizer	*to say*	digo (first person)	→ Diga!	*Say!*
estar	*to be*		→ Esteja!	*Be!*

Empurre o carro, por favor.	*Push the car, please.*
Venda tudo!	*Sell everything!*
Abra a loja às oito.	*Open the shop at eight.*
Venha comigo.	*Come with me.*

The *vocês* form, or plural command

As above, the **vocês** form goes into the subjunctive, in the third person plural. Its formation is as described above.

lavar	to wash	lavam (third person plural)	Lavem!	Wash!
beber	to drink	bebem (third person)	Bebam!	Drink!
abrir	to open	abrem (third person)	Abram!	Open!
seguir	to follow	sigo (first person)	Sigam!	Follow!
saber	to know		Saibam!	Know!

Esperem aqui.	*Wait here.*
Escolham o que querem.	*Choose what you want.*
Subam as escadas.	*Go up the steps.*
Ponham as malas ali.	*Put the cases there.*

Negative commands

All commands in the negative (i.e. telling someone **not** to do something) use the appropriate subjunctive form. Don't forget to move the position of any reflexive pronouns if you are using a reflexive verb.

esperar	to wait	Não esperes! (tu)	*Don't wait!*
correr	to run	Não corrais! (vós)	*Do not run!*
abrir	to open	Não abra! (você)	*Don't open!*
trazer	to bring	Não tragam! (vocês)	*Don't bring!*
ter	to have	Não tenha! (o senhor)	*Don't have!*

Não te sentes perto de mim.	*Don't sit near me.*
Não deiteis lixo na rua.	*Don't throw litter in the street.*
Não lhe dê o livro.	*Don't give her the book.*
Nunca atravessem sem ajuda.	*Never cross without help.*
Não subas agora.	*Don't go up now.*
Não feche a loja até à uma.	*Don't close the shop until one o'clock.*

Polite commands

Requests can be softened by using the construction **fazer favor + de** + infinitive.

Faz favor de abrir a porta.	*Please open the door.* (tu)
Faça favor de não falar tão alto.	*Please don't speak so loud.* (polite, singular)
Façam favor de me ajudar	*Please help me.* (plural)

The same type of polite request can be made by using **querer** (*to want, wish*) + infinitive, or **ter a bondade de** (*to have the kindness to*) + infinitive.

Quer abrir a janela para mim?	*Would you mind opening the window for me?*
Queres ajudar o teu irmão?	*Would you help your brother?*
Tenham a bondade de preencher esta ficha.	*Would you be so kind as to fill in this form?*

You also saw in Unit 19 how infinitives can be used to convey public instructions, especially on notices.

Não mergulhar!	*No diving (do not dive)!*

In everyday Portuguese, it is also very common to 'tell' someone to do something by 'asking' them by using the present tense, especially with people you know.

Fazes isto para mim?	*Will you do this for me? (Do this for me, will you?)*
Pões a mesa, sim?	*Set the table, will you?*

Exercises

A In each sentence form the correct command according to the guidance given.

1 **Comer** (tu) .... todos os vegetais!
2 **Limpar** (você) .... os sapatos!
3 Não **falar** (vocês) .... tão alto!
4 **Cantar** (vós) .... com alegria!
5 **Comprar** (você) .... um gelado para mim!
6 Não **abrir** (tu) .... a janela!
7 **Dormir** (vocês) .... bem!
8 Não **mentir** (tu) ....!
9 **Votar** (vós) .... para os vossos direitos!
10 Não **escrever** (você) .... no livro!

B Match up the four pictures illustrating how to change your telephone service provider with the instructions below.

1    **2**

3    **4**

a Fale.
b Levante o auscultador.
c Pouse o auscultador.
d Marque 1010, seguido do número pretendido.

Grammar in context

Here are recent driving safety instructions issued by the Portuguese government.

A

Lembre-se que o andar depressa
nem sempre significa chegar
mais cedo.
Respeite os limites de velocidade.

B

Se conduzir não beba;
deixe a comemoração para a
chegada.

C

Por amor às crianças… utilize
sempre a protecção adequada.

D

O cansaço é perigoso…
para chegar e voltar pare de
2 em 2 horas

1 What should you respect?
2 Is it advisable to drink and drive in Portugal?
3 What is the infinitive of the verb used in box C?
4 How often are you recommended to have a rest from driving?

37

irregular verbs

In this unit you will learn
- the most common irregular verbs in Portuguese, in the present, preterite and imperfect tenses

Grammar in focus

As the term suggests, irregular verbs are those that do not follow the normal pattern for endings in some, or all, tenses. This unit will illustrate a dozen of the most commonly used irregular verbs, across the present, preterite and imperfect tenses, with examples. For more comprehensive coverage, refer to the verb tables on pages 263–71.

Present

dar *to give*	dizer *to say*	estar *to be*	fazer *to do / make*
(eu) dou	digo	estou	faço
(tu) dás	dizes	estás	fazes
(ele etc.) dá	diz	está	faz
(nós) damos	dizemos	estamos	fazemos
(vós) dais	dizeis	estais	fazeis
(eles etc.) dão	dizem	estão	fazem

haver *to have*	ir *to go*	poder *to be able*	pôr *to put*
hei	vou	posso	ponho
hás	vais	podes	pões
há	vai	pode	põe
havemos	vamos	podemos	pomos
haveis	ides	podeis	pondes
hão	vão	podem	põem

ser *to be*	ter *to have*	ver *to see*	vir *to come*
sou	tenho	vejo	venho
és	tens	vês	vens
é	tem	vê	vem
somos	temos	vemos	vimos
sois	tendes	vedes	vindes
são	têm	vêem	vêm

Be particularly careful with **ver** and **vir** – they always catch people out.

Sempre dou roupa velha aos pobres.	*I always give old clothes to the poor.*
Onde estás?	*Where are you?*
Ele há-de ser famoso.	*He'll be famous.*
Não podemos entender.	*We cannot understand.*

Preterite

dar *to give*	dizer *to say*	estar *to be*	fazer *to do / make*
(eu) dei	disse	estive	fiz
(tu) deste	disseste	estiveste	fizeste
(ele etc.) deu	disse	esteve	fez
(nós) demos	dissemos	estivemos	fizemos
(vós) destes	dissestes	estivestes	fizestes
(eles etc.) deram	disseram	estiveram	fizeram

haver *to have*	ir *to go*	poder *to be able*	pôr *to put*
houve	fui	pude	pus
houveste	foste	pudeste	puseste
houve	foi	pôde	pôs
houvemos	fomos	pudemos	pusemos
houvestes	fostes	pudestes	pusestes
houveram	foram	puderam	puseram

ser *to be*	ter *to have*	ver *to see*	vir *to come*
fui	tive	vi	vim
foste	tiveste	viste	vieste
foi	teve	viu	veio
fomos	tivemos	vimos	viemos
fostes	tivestes	vistes	viestes
foram	tiveram	viram	vieram

Note that the preterite of **ser** and **ir** is the same. Watch out for **ver** and **vir** again. Otherwise, there are definitely patterns you can spot to help you with your learning.

Não disseram nada.	*They didn't say anything.*
Vós fizestes tudo para o Senhor.	*You did everything for the Lord.*
Onde foste ontem?	*Where did you go yesterday?*
O Miguel pôs a mesa.	*Miguel set the table.*

Imperfect

dar *to give*	dizer *to say*	estar *to be*	fazer *to do / make*
(eu) dava	dizia	estava	fazia
(tu) davas	dizias	estavas	fazias
(ele etc.) dava	dizia	estava	fazia
(nós) dávamos	dizíamos	estávamos	fazíamos
(vós) dáveis	dizíeis	estáveis	fazíeis
(eles etc.) davam	diziam	estavam	faziam

haver *to have*	ir *to go*	poder *to be able*	pôr *to put*
havia	ia	podia	punha
havias	ias	podias	punhas
havia	ia	podia	punha
havíamos	íamos	podíamos	púnhamos
havíeis	íeis	podíeis	púnheis
haviam	iam	podiam	punham

ser *to be*	ter *to have*	ver *to see*	vir *to come*
era	tinha	via	vinha
eras	tinhas	vias	vinhas
era	tinha	via	vinha
éramos	tínhamos	víamos	vínhamos
éreis	tínheis	víeis	vínheis
eram	tinham	viam	vinham

Era uma vida muito corrida.	*It was a very busy life.*
Ela via a televisão enquanto ele dormia.	*She was watching TV whilst he was sleeping.*
Não tínhamos suficiente para entrar.	*We didn't have enough to go in.*
Antigamente sempre vinhas à minha casa para almoçar.	*In the past you always used to come to my house for lunch.*

Exercises

A Complete these sentences by correctly forming the irregular verbs. Numbers 1–4 are in the present, 5–7 in the preterite, and 8–10 in the imperfect.

1 Eu .... na cozinha. (estar)
2 Tu .... ao cinema no sábado? (ir)
3 O marido dela .... engenheiro. (ser)
4 Sim, nós .... no carro. (vir)
5 Quando .... vocês a festa? (fazer)
6 Eu não .... sair. (poder)
7 Tu .... muita sorte. (ter)
8 Você nunca .... dinheiro aos pobres. (dar)
9 .... muitas pessoas na rua. (haver)
10 Nós .... a mesa. (pôr)

B Place the verbs in the box in the correct column, according to their tenses.

Agora	Ontem	Antigamente

> estávamos   tínheis   dizemos   podes
> haviam   houveram   sei   dou   vieste   foste
> põe   punha   hás   pudeste   fazias   vou   disse
> fiz   pode   faz   fazes   estou   viste   fostes
> estivemos   têm   tinha   tive

Grammar in context

In the north of Portugal you can visit the Museu dos Carros Antigos (*Museum of Vintage Cars*). Which irregular verbs are used in the flyer for the museum?

> ### MUSEU DOS CARROS ANTIGOS
>
> Venha ver os carros do século passado. O museu foi criado em 1985 – pode ser visitado às terças, quartas, e quintas. Fechado feriados.
>
> 2,00 €

38

ser and estar

In this unit you will learn
- how to form and use the verbs ser and estar and the differences between them

Grammar in focus

In Portuguese, there are two verbs *to be* (*I am, you are, he is,* etc.), each used in specific circumstances. The full conjugations for the verbs are given in the verb tables on pages 263–71; the present tense is listed here again as a reminder.

	ser	estar	
eu	sou	estou	*I am*
tu	és	estás	*you are*
ele, ela, você	é	está	*s/he / it is, you are*
nós	somos	estamos	*we are*
vós	sois	estais	*you (pl.) are*
eles etc.	são	estão	*they, you (pl.) are*

The verb **ficar** (*to stay, be / be located, become*) is also often used, in expressions such as **Onde fica o banco?** (*Where is the bank?*).

Ser – 'permanent' conditions

- Nationality

  Sou inglesa.   *I am English.*

- Professions / status / nature

  Ela é engenheira.   *She is an engineer.* [NB no word for *a*]

  Isto é um gato.   *This is a cat.*
  Nós somos colegas.   *We are colleagues.*

- Marital status

  És casado?   *Are you married?*

- Origin

  De onde são?   Somos de   *Where are you from?*
       Campinas.   *We are from Campinas.*

- Possession

  De quem é o livro?   *Whose is the book?*
       É meu.   *It's mine.*

- Time (see Unit 16)

  São oito e meia.   *It's 8.30.*
  Hoje é sábado.   *Today is Saturday.*

- What something is made of

Esta caixa é de prata.   *This box is made of silver.*

- Geographical location

O Brasil é na América do Sul.   *Brazil is in South America.*
O castelo é no centro da   *The castle is in the town*
  cidade.   *centre.*

- With adjectives, to describe permanent and inherent characteristics

Elas são bonitas.   *They are pretty.*
Sou baixinha!   *I'm a shorty* (shortish)*!*

- In impersonal expressions

É incrível.   *It's incredible.*
Era possível.   *It was possible.*

- Permanent weather features/climate

Na Inglaterra o tempo é   *In England the weather is*
  variável.   *changeable.*

(Temporary weather conditions use **estar**, **fazer** and **haver**, amongst other verbs.)

- Passive sentences (see Unit 39)

A janela foi partida pelos   *The window was broken by*
meninos.   *the lads.*

Estar – temporary states or conditions; things that can change

- Position or location

Onde estão os pratos?   *Where are the plates?*
Ela está em Paris.   *She is in Paris.*

- Weather

Hoje está muito frio.   *Today it's very cold.*

- With adjectives – temporary states, moods, results of change etc.

Como estás?   Estou mais   *How are you?   I'm so–so.*
  ou menos.
O chá já está frio.   *The tea's cold now.*
Estamos felizes por termos   *We are happy because we've*
  ganhado a lotaria.   *won the lottery.*

- As a substitute for **ter**, with **com** (see Unit 30)

Estou com sono = Tenho sono.	*I am tired.*
Estavam com medo = Tinham medo.	*They were afraid.*

- In continuous tenses (see Unit 34)

Está a fazer compras.	*She is doing the shopping.*
Estávamos nadando.	*We were swimming.*

Sometimes it's tricky to remember which verb to use, especially when you may be able to argue a case both ways. In that situation, you may be justified in using either, depending on the viewpoint.

Ela é bonita.	*She is a pretty girl.*
Ela está bonita.	*She is well-turned out / looking nice* (at the moment).

Exercises

A **Ser** or **estar**? Decide whether the correct verb is used in each example. If the verb is incorrect, give the correct form.

                                   ✓/✗   Correct verb

1 A mesa está limpa.
2 Não está bom tempo.
3 Eu estou francês.
4 A minha mãe não é em casa.
5 Como estás? Estou bem, obrigada.
6 Ela está professora.
7 O bolo está em cima da mesa.
8 Eles são do norte.
9 Nós somos cansados hoje.
10 Esta caixa está de madeira.

B Complete the sentences with the correct form of either **ser** or **estar**.

1 O meu café .... frio.
2 O banco .... fechado.
3 Nós .... em São Paulo.
4 Eles .... italianos.
5 A colher .... suja.

6 Os seus sapatos .... muito sujos.
7 Aquela casa .... muito pequena.
8 Onde .... as malas?
9 Ela .... inteligente.
10 Eu .... um pouco cansado.

C Memory test! Without looking back at the grammar explanations, see if you can match each category to the correct verb, **ser** or **estar**. Then check back to see how much you've remembered, and focus more on the bits you struggled to recall. The answers to this activity are not in the Key.

professions   temporary weather

location or position   nationality

possession   changeable states, moods

SER

ESTAR

marital status   in place of **ter**   materials

inherent characteristics   time

continuous tenses   geographical location

Grammar in context

This verse from a song by Portuguese singer Rui Veloso contains four examples of the verb **ser**. Match up the ones you find with the English below.

> Porque é que tudo é incerto
> Não pode ser sempre assim
> Se não fosse o rock and roll
> O que seria de mim?
>
> [From: Rui Veloso, *Não há estrelas no céu*]

1 (If) it were (not) for...
2 (It cannot) be...
3 is
4 (what) would be

39

the passive

In this unit you will learn
- how to use the passive voice in Portuguese, and convert sentences from active to passive
- ways of avoiding the passive

Grammar in focus

An ordinary sentence is made up of a subject, a verb, an object, and whatever adjectives, adverbs, or other types of words are necessary to give any further appropriate information. A sentence with the word order subject–verb–object is said to be in the *active voice*. In the active voice, the subject performs the action of the verb. However, the word order can be changed without altering the meaning of the sentence. If the subject then receives the action of the verb, or is acted upon by the object, the sentence is said to belong to the *passive voice*. In English you would expect to see phrases such as 'the books are sold by that man', or 'the village was invaded'.

In Portuguese, the passive voice is formed with **ser**, in any tense, and the past participle of the verb. The past participle agrees with the subject of the verb in number (singular or plural) and gender (masculine or feminine). The person or thing carrying out the action, known as 'the agent' is introduced by **por** (*by*) and its combinations (see Unit 9). It is not always necessary to show the agent.

The boy broke the window.	O menino partiu a janela.	ACTIVE

The window was broken
  by the boy.
	A janela foi partida
	  pelo menino.
		PASSIVE

The actual sense hasn't changed at all; there has just been a shift in emphasis. The passive is particularly useful when the 'agent' is not known:

During the night the window
  was broken.
	Durante a noite a janela foi
	  partida.

Later in this unit you will see other ways of conveying what has happened, which do not involve the use of the passive.

Ser + past participle

Active	Passive

Todos os alunos respeitam
  o professor.
	O professor é respeitado por
	  todos os alunos.

All the pupils respect the
  teacher.
	The teacher is respected by all
	  the pupils.

Ana escolheu este filme.	Este filme foi escolhido por Ana.
Ana chose this film.	*This film was chosen by Ana.*

Active	Passive
As filhas vão lavar os cães.	Os cães vão ser lavados pelas filhas.
The daughters are going to wash the dogs.	*The dogs are going to be washed by the daughters.*
Sílvia tinha vendido todas as cadeiras.	Todas as cadeiras tinham sido vendidas por Sílvia.
Sílvia had sold all the chairs.	*All the chairs had been sold by Sílvia.*

The agent can be omitted if it is unknown or indefinite.

O país foi invadido.	*The country was invaded.*
A senhora tinha sido atacada.	*The lady had been attacked.*

Estar + past participle

Estar may be used with a past participle to describe a state resulting from an action. Again, the past participle agrees in number and gender, just as an adjective would, and can be used with any tense.

A farmácia está fechada.	*The pharmacy is closed.*
Os barcos estavam afundados.	*The boats were sunk (i.e. under the water).*

Remember that some verbs have two past participles: one to be used with the auxiliary verb **ter**, the other for use with **ser** and **estar** (see Unit 31).

Reflexive substitute for the passive

Often, the reflexive pronoun **se** is used to convey the passive, particularly when the subject of the verb is unknown, undetermined, or irrelevant to comprehension of the phrase. It is seen on many public signs and notices. **Se** is placed next to the verb according to the normal rules of positioning. The verb is in the active voice in the third person, either singular or plural, depending on the context.

Aqui fala-se inglês.	*English is spoken here.*
Aluga-se terreno.	*Land to rent.*
Não se ouviram as notícias.	*The news was not heard.*

Although the phrase **Aluga-se terreno** translates literally as *Land rents itself*, its meaning is the same as *Land to rent* or even

We have land to rent. These reflexive sentences can often be rendered in English by using *they, we* or *people*. Unfortunately, it is now commonplace in signs and notices for the construction to be used incorrectly, with the verb in the singular, when it should be in the plural. A very common notice is:

Vende-se apartamentos.   *Apartments for sale.*

Strictly speaking, the verb should be **vendem-se**, as the subject is plural (**apartamentos**). There is divided debate now about what is right and wrong (traditionalists frown on the incorrect usage, others accept it as a sign of evolution!). Have a look around you the next time you are in a Portuguese-speaking country, and see what evidence you can find yourself. Often the same meaning can be conveyed by simply using the third person plural:

Um preço foi combinado.   *A price was agreed.*
Combinaram um preço.   *They agreed a price.*

Impersonal use of se

Se can be used with the third person singular to express an indefinite subject (*it, they, one* or *you*). This is a similar concept to the French use of **on** (*one*).

Como se diz isto em   *How do you say this in*
    português?   *Portuguese?*
Nunca se sabe o que vai   *One never knows what's going*
    acontecer.   *to happen.*
Como se escreve o seu nome?   *How do you write your name?*

Exercises

A Change the active sentences into passive constructions. The beginning of each one has been done for you.

1 A Maria pagou o jantar. O jantar...
2 Todos os turistas adoram os lagos. Os lagos...
3 O Benfica ganhou a partida. A partida...
4 O João levou o carro. O carro,.,
5 Vão abrir uma nova discoteca. Uma nova discoteca...
6 Assaltaram o Banco do Brasil. O Banco do Brasil...
7 Perderam os cães na floresta. Os cães...
8 Eu fiz o trabalho. O trabalho...
9 O Luís Figo vai inaugurar o concurso. O concurso...
10 A música acordou as senhoras. As senhoras...

B Say what has happened in each picture, by describing the result of the action, using **estar** + past participle. Choose verbs from the box.

limpar	fazer	abrir	fechar	salvar	assinar
	pintar	cortar			

Grammar in context

Look at this sign in Silves castle in the Algarve.

> Silves foi conquistada por Abd-al-Aziz
> em 713, tendo permanecido sob
> administração islâmica até meados do
> século XIII, altura em que foi tomada por
> D. Paio Peres Correia, mestre da Ordem
> de Santiago. Todavia, o rei D. Sancho I,
> ajudado por Cruzados, que se dirigiam à
> Terra Santa, haviam conquistado a cidade,
> em 1189, mas os Cristãos só nela
> permaneceram cerca de dois anos.

1 In what year was the castle conquered, and by whom?
2 It remained under Islamic administration until the middle of
  the thirteenth century, when it was taken back by whom? To
  which chivalric order did he belong?
3 **Silves foi conquistada por... / Foi tomada por D. (Dom) ...**
  How could you re-write these two clauses in the active voice,
  using the verbs **conquistar** and **tomar**?

40

tenses of the subjunctive

In this unit you will learn
- how to form the subjunctive in different tenses

Grammar in focus

Up to now we have concerned ourselves with verb formations in the 'indicative mood'. The subjunctive mood is another set of structures used in various tenses, for such circumstances as the giving of commands; the expression of desire, hope, and influence; after certain conjunctions; and in general, whenever situations described appear to be doubtful or uncertain.

It is not surprising that many, if not all, learners, throw up their hands in horror at the sheer mention of the word 'subjunctive'. Having spent precious hours mastering various sets of verb endings, it is frustrating to be presented with a completely new range. But, with careful practice, you can learn to detect when a subjunctive is called for. Paying attention to the presence of the subjunctive while reading newspapers or magazines, to see how and when it is used, can be an especially helpful practice.

In this unit the formation of the subjunctive in different tenses is given, then, in the following units, those occasions in which it should be used are described.

Tenses of the subjunctive

1 Present
2 Imperfect
3 Future
4 Present perfect
5 Pluperfect (past perfect)
6 Future perfect

Present subjunctive

With the exception of the irregular verbs **dar, estar, ser, ir, haver, saber** and **querer**, all other verbs, including any which may change their spelling (see Units 21 and 22), form the present subjunctive in the same way. The stem is that of the first person singular of the present indicative, and the following endings are added:

	-ar verbs	*-er* verbs	*-ir* verbs
eu	+ e	+ a	+ a
tu	+ es	+ as	+ as
ele / ela / você	+ e	+ a	+ a
nós	+ emos	+ amos	+ amos
vós	+ eis	+ ais	+ ais
eles / elas / vocês	+ em	+ am	+ am

Can you spot the patterns? In fact, the endings of the present tense have crossed over from:

$$-AR \longleftrightarrow \begin{cases} -ER \\ -IR \end{cases}$$

falar	comer	partir
1st person = **falo**	1st person = **como**	1st person = **parto**
fale	coma	parta
fales	comas	partas
fale	coma	parta
falemos	comamos	partamos
faleis	comais	partais
falem	comam	partam

In the above examples of regular verbs, the stem used happens to be the same as the normal stem for the present indicative. However, if we look at a verb such as **pedir** (*to ask for*), the normal stem taken from the infinitive is **ped-** but the first person singular of the indicative is **peço**. Consequently, the present subjunctive becomes:

pedir   First person singular: peço
peça   peçamos
peças   peçais
peça   peçam

This illustrates the importance of using the stem of the first person singular, instead of relying on that of the infinitive.

The next chapter will deal more fully with the uses of the subjunctive. Following are some examples in the present tense, simply to illustrate the form.

Esperamos que tenhas uma boa festa.	*We hope that you have a good party.*
Talvez eu compre uma casa.	*Perhaps I'll buy a house.*
Prefere que a minha irmã faça o trabalho?	*Would you rather my sister did the work?* (lit. *Do you prefer that my sister does the work?*)

Imperfect subjunctive

The imperfect subjunctive is formed by adding the following endings onto the stem of the third person plural of the preterite (indicative). Again, following this rule is particularly important where irregular verbs are concerned.

	-*ar* verbs	-*er* verbs	-*ir* verbs
eu	+ asse	+ esse	+ isse
tu	+ asses	+ esses	+ isses
ele / ela / você	+ asse	+ esse	+ isse
nós	+ ássemos	+ êssemos	+ íssemos
vós	+ ásseis	+ êsseis	+ ísseis
eles / elas / vocês	+ assem	+ essem	+ issem

falar	comer	partir
3rd pers. pret. = falaram	3rd pers. pret. = comeram	3rd pers. pret. = partiram
falasse	comesse	partisse
falasses	comesses	partisses
falasse	comesse	partisse
falássemos	comêssemos	partíssemos
falásseis	comêsseis	partísseis
falassem	comessem	partissem

As for the present subjunctive, there are a number of uses for the imperfect subjunctive, which will be dealt with more fully later.

A Margarida pediu que nós a ajudássemos.	*Margarida asked us to help her.*
Mandaram-lhe que assinasse o documento.	*They ordered him to sign the document.*
Se ganhasses muito dinheiro podias comprar o carro.	*If you won a lot of money you'd be able to buy the car.*

Future subjunctive

The future subjunctive is also based on the stem of the third person plural of the preterite indicative, onto which are added the following endings:

	-*ar* verbs	-*er* verbs	-*ir* verbs
eu	+ ar	+ er	+ ir
tu	+ ares	+ eres	+ ires
ele / ela / você	+ ar	+ er	+ ir
nós	+ armos	+ ermos	+ irmos
vós	+ ardes	+ erdes	+ irdes
eles / elas / vocês	+ arem	+ erem	+ irem

falar	comer	partir
3rd pers. pret = **falaram** stem = **fal**	3rd pers. pret = **comeram** stem = **com**	3rd pers. pret = **partiram** stem = **part**
falar	comer	partir
falares	comeres	partires
falar	comer	partir
falarmos	comermos	partirmos
falardes	comerdes	partirdes
falarem	comerem	partirem

Don't be fooled into thinking that the first and third person singular is simply the infinitive, although in regular verbs it does have the same form. Compare with an irregular verb:

fazer → third person preterite = **fizeram** → stem = **fiz** → future subj. = **fizer**

The future subjunctive is used when referring to indefinite or hypothetical future situations. In this context, it follows such conjunctions as **quando** (*when*), **assim que** (*as soon as*), **se** (*if*), **logo que** (*as soon as*), **conforme** (*depending on whether*), and **enquanto** (*while*), among others. In English we are more likely to use a simple present tense in these circumstances.

Quando chegarmos, vamos fazer um chazinho?	*When we arrive, shall we make a nice cup of tea?*
Só vais à praia quando terminares os estudos.	*You're only going to the beach when you finish your studies.*
Se vier o meu primo, diga-lhe que estou em casa.	*If my cousin comes, tell him that I'm at home.*

Present perfect subjunctive

For all verbs this is formed with the present subjunctive of the verb **ter**, plus the past participle of the main verb.

comprar + first person singular present subj. of **ter**: **tenho** = **tenha**

tenha comprado	tenhamos comprado
tenhas comprado	tenhais comprado
tenha comprado	tenham comprado

Duvido que tenha comprado a casa.	*I doubt that you have bought the house.*

| Não pensas que é estranho que eles não tenham vindo ao trabalho? | *Don't you think it strange that they have not come to work?* |
| Talvez tenhamos comido demais, não acham? | *Perhaps we have eaten too much, don't you think?* |

Pluperfect (past perfect) subjunctive

For all verbs this is formed with the imperfect subjunctive of the verb **ter**, plus the past participle of the main verb.

comer third person plural of **ter**: **tiveram** → imperfect subj. = **tivesse**

tivesse comido	tivéssemos comido
tivesses comido	tivésseis comido
tivesse comido	tivessem comido

Se tivesses comido o pequeno almoço, não terias ficado com fome agora.	*If you had eaten breakfast, you wouldn't be hungry* (have become hungry) *now.*
Souberam a verdade, embora ela tivesse negado tudo.	*They found out the truth, even though she had denied everything.*
Achei incrível que elas tivessem gasto tanto dinheiro.	*I thought it incredible that they had spent so much money.*

Future perfect subjunctive

For all verbs this is formed with the future subjunctive of **ter**, plus the past participle of the main verb.

abrir third person plural of **ter**: **tiveram** → future subj. = **tiver**

tiver aberto	tivermos aberto
tiveres aberto	tiverdes aberto
tiver aberto	tiverem aberto

Se não tiver comido tudo, não vai sair.	*If you have not eaten it all, you're not going out.*
Quando tiveres terminado o curso, o que vais fazer?	*When you have finished the course, what are you going to do?*
Assim que tivermos chegado, compraremos um jornal.	*As soon as we have arrived, we'll buy a paper.*

Exercises

A Complete the table with the appropriate forms of the verbs indicated.

Present subjunctive

	eu	tu	ele / você	nós	eles
pintar	pinte	....	....	....	....
beber	....	....	....	....	....
partir	....	....	....	....	....
fazer	....	....	....	....	....

Imperfect subjunctive

	eu	tu	ele / você	nós	eles
estudar	....	estudasses	....	....	....
correr	....	....	....	....	....
ter	....	....	....	....	....
dormir	....	....	....	....	....

B In each example identify the tense of the subjunctive, the person, the infinitive of the main verb, and what the infinitive means. The first is done as an example.

1 tenhas comido = present perfect / 2nd person singular / **comer** / *to eat*
2 façam
3 eu trabalhasse
4 abrirdes
5 ele tivesse bebido
6 tivermos feito
7 decidas
8 comprarmos
9 tivesse doido
10 viessem

Grammar in context

FORA COM AS ARANHAS

Para que as teias de aranha não voltem a aparecer, espalhe no local onde elas se encontram laca de cabelo. Experimente!

In this useful suggestion, from a magazine, for getting rid of spiders, **voltem, espalhe** and **experimente** are all examples of verbs in the present subjunctive. What are the infinitives?

41

subjunctive: emotion, doubt, desire, influence

In this unit you will learn
• how to use the subjunctive to express emotion, doubt, desire or influence and which verbs to use

Grammar in focus

The subjunctive is used after verbs that fall into this category. The verb in the subordinate clause – that part of the sentence that generally follows the word **que** (*that*) – is in the subjunctive, i.e. the subjunctive is not in the verb introducing the emotion, but in the one resulting in that emotion, wish etc. Verbs commonly used to express influence (desire / wishes / orders) include:

não admitir (que)	*to not allow*
aconselhar (que)	*to advise*
consentir (que)	*to consent to*
desejar (que)	*to want, desire*
dizer (que)	*to say, tell*
esperar (que)	*to hope, wish*
implorar (que)	*to implore, beg*
mandar (que)	*to order*
negar (que)	*to deny*
pedir (que)	*to ask for*
permitir (que)	*to allow, permit*
persuadir (que)	*to persuade*
precisar (que)	*to need*
preferir (que)	*to prefer*
proibir (que)	*to forbid*
querer (que)	*to wish, want*

Espero que tenham boas férias.	*I hope that you have a good holiday.*
Queres que te ajude?	*Do you want me to help you?*
Preferíamos que não o tocasse.	*We would prefer that you didn't touch it.*
Implorou ao ladrão que não levasse o gato.	*She begged the thief not to take her cat.*
Porque negas que tenhas mentido?	*Why do you deny that you've lied?*

Note: If the subject of the verb expressing desire etc., is the same as that of the second verb – that is, if the desire expressed relates to oneself – the infinitive construction is used.

Espero que visite Roma.	*I hope you visit Rome.*
Espero visitar Roma.	*I hope to visit Rome.*

Verbs expressing emotion

All types of emotions expressed towards another party, such as anger, happiness, sadness or fear, place the verb following **que** in the subjunctive as above. Typical verbs of emotion include:

alegrar-se (que)	*to be glad*
estranhar (que)	*to be surprised*
sentir (que)	*to feel; to feel sorry*
temer (que)	*to fear*
ter pena de (que)	*to be sorry (for)*
ter medo (que)	*to be frightened*

Sinto muito que a tua filha não esteja bem.	*I'm very sorry that your daughter isn't well.*
Ela temia que houvesse / estivesse alguém na casa.	*She was afraid that there might be someone in the house.*
Estranhamos que ela tenha tanto dinheiro.	*We are surprised that she has so much money.*

Verbs expressing doubt

ter dúvidas (que)	*to have doubts that*
duvidar (que)	*to doubt*

Temos dúvidas que custe tanto.	*We doubt that it costs so much.*
Duvidava que ele viesse.	*She doubted that he would come.*

Exercises

A Choose the correct verb form for each sentence.

1 Espero que se sente / sinta melhor.
2 Disse-lhe que fosse / foi embora.
3 Não queremos que façam / fazem um jantar.
4 Alegrou-se que ela ganhou / tivesse ganho.
5 Temiam que nós tivéssemos ido / tínhamos ido.
6 Duvido que mores / moras aqui.
7 Esperamos ver / que vejamos o filme hoje.
8 Proíbe que o filho saia / sai à noite.
9 Mandaram-lhes que voltassem / voltaram ao trabalho.
10 Sinto muito que não estejam / estão bem.

B Ten verbs used with the subjunctive are hidden in the wordsearch. Can you find them all? Here is the list in English:

to advise   to feel (sorry)   to need   to be glad
to forbid   to hope / wish   to be surprised   to say
to deny   to fear

A	C	O	N	S	E	L	H	A	R
B	C	D	E	E	G	H	R	L	I
L	M	N	O	N	Q	E	S	E	B
V	W	X	Y	T	Z	B	C	G	I
F	G	H	I	I	K	L	M	R	O
R	Q	R	D	R	U	V	W	A	R
E	A	R	A	S	I	C	E	R	P
M	K	G	M	N	O	P	Q	S	S
E	S	P	E	R	A	R	A	E	C
T	R	A	H	N	A	R	T	S	E

Grammar in context

As a country concerned not to contract Foot and Mouth disease
(**a febre aftosa**), Portugal regularly issues warning leaflets to
visitors arriving from countries where an outbreak may have
occurred. Which verb calls for the subjunctive after it, and what
does it mean?

Solicitamos que informe o **Veterinário Inspector / Oficial
da Alfândega**, nos seguintes casos:

• Se transportar na sua bagagem qualquer produto de
origem animal, para consumir durante a viagem, para
oferecer como presente ou para fins comerciais.

ou

• Se nas duas semanas anteriores visitou alguma
exploração com **bovinos**, **ovinos**, **caprinos** ou **suínos**,
no seu país de origem ou no decorrer da sua viagem.

42

subjunctive: impersonal expressions and verbs of opinion

In this unit you will learn
- the use of the subjunctive in impersonal expressions such as é possível que and é necessário que
- how to use the subjunctive in negative expressions of thinking and believing

Grammar in focus

The subjunctive is used after expressions which are termed 'impersonal'; in English, these expressions usually begin with *it*. The expressions may be in any tense, although in practice you will find them mostly in the present (with references to actions generally in the future), and imperfect (for actions in the past). Remember to change the tense of the verb in the subjunctive accordingly. Here is a selection of the more common expressions. They all take the word **que** (*that*) after them, and it is the verb following **que** that goes into the subjunctive.

Impersonal expressions

é provável (que)	*it is probable*
é possível (que)	*it is possible*
é incrível (que)	*it is incredible*
é estranho (que)	*it is strange*
é lógico (que)	*it is logical*
é natural (que)	*it is natural*
é bom (que)	*it is good*
é importante (que)	*it is important*
é necessário (que)	*it is necessary*
é preciso (que)	*it is necessary*
é melhor (que)	*it is better / best*
é suficiente (que)	*it is sufficient / enough*
é conveniente (que)	*it is convenient*
convém (que)	*it is convenient / appropriate*
basta (que)	*it is enough*

É provável que ela chegue primeiro.	*It's probable that she will arrive first. (She'll probably arrive first.)*
É lógico que não queiram fazer a viagem.	*It's logical that they don't want to make the journey.*
Era necessário que tu ficasses fora do país.	*It was necessary for you to stay (that you stayed) outside the country.*

When the following expressions indicate true or clear-cut situations, the verbs are in the indicative mood. However, when they are used in the negative, as contrary to fact or suggesting doubt, the following verb goes into the subjunctive again.

é verdade (que)	*it is true*
é evidente (que)	*it is evident*
é certo (que)	*it is true; it is certain*

| é óbvio (que) | *it is obvious* |
| é manifesto (que) | *it is clear* |

| É verdade que ela estuda muito. | *It's true that she studies a lot.* INDICATIVE |
| Não é verdade que ela estude muito. | *It's not true...* SUBJUNCTIVE |

Impersonal expressions can, of course, also be used with the infinitive, if the dependent verb has no definite subject.

| É possível comprar sapatos ao mercado. | *It's possible to buy shoes at the market.* |
| Não é natural trabalhar tanto. | *It's not natural to work so much.* |

Verbs of opinion

The verbs of thinking and believing take the indicative mood when in the affirmative, but in the negative assume the subjunctive after them. There are different ways you can offer your thoughts and opinions in Portuguese:

achar (que)	*to think / reckon that*
crer (que)	*to believe that*
julgar (que)	*to think / judge that*
pensar (que)	*to think that*
parecer (que)	*to seem* (to one) *that*

Acho que este é um bom filme.	*I think this is a good film.* INDICATIVE
Não acho que este seja um bom filme.	*I don't think this ...* SUBJUNCTIVE
Julgávamos que o hotel era muito caro.	*We thought that the hotel was very expensive.*
Não julgávamos que o hotel fosse muito caro.	*We did not think that the hotel...*

Special expressions

These special expressions employ both the present and future subjunctives – the present in the first verb, and the future in the second one:

seja o que for	*whatever it may be*
seja como for	*however it may be*
seja quanto for	*however much it may be*
seja quando for	*whenever it may be*

seja quem for	*whoever it may be*
esteja onde estiver	*wherever I / he / she / you or it may be*
venha o que vier	*come what may*
custe o que custar	*at whatever cost*

This construction can be applied to many other verbs. It can also be used to describe past circumstances and events, with both verbs in the imperfect subjunctive.

| fosse o que fosse | *whatever it might be / have been* |
| estivesse onde estivesse | *wherever he / she / you it might be / have been* |

Exercises

A Re-arrange the words in each example to make complete sentences.

1 é venham que provável eles tarde mais
2 verdade muito trabalhas é tu que
3 a achamos boa que foi comida
4 venha vou que o vier Brasil ao
5 falasse o que incrível Nelson era assim
6 tivessem era feito que evidente eles não isto
7 melhor é não nada dizer
8 penso doente estejas não tu que

B Match up the Portuguese and English expressions.

1	é possível	a	we don't think that
2	era estranho	b	it's enough that
3	é bom	c	it was strange
4	é preciso	d	I believe that
5	era conveniente	e	it's necessary
6	basta que	f	wherever they may be
7	não é certo	g	it was convenient
8	creio que	h	it's possible
9	estejam onde estiverem	i	it's not certain
10	não julgamos que	j	it's good

Grammar in context

Look how the Brazilian singer Roberto Carlos uses a subjunctive expression in the third line of this verse of one of his slower songs, *Toda vã filosofia* (*All vain philosophy*):

> *Por isso insisto em cultivar*
> *Os meus sonhos, minha fé*
> *Esteja aonde eu estiver*
> *Creio em você*
> *Eu estou em segurança.*

sonhos	*dreams*
fé	*faith*
segurança	*security / safety*

What does the subjunctive expression mean?

43

subjunctive: conjunctions and hypothesis

In this unit you will learn
- some conjunctions which take the subjunctive
- expressing hypothesis with talvez and oxalá + subjunctive
- some other special expressions using the subjunctive

Grammar in focus

There are a variety of conjunctions (words which join parts of sentences together, or begin phrases) and expressions of hypothesis (assumption) that are followed by a verb in the subjunctive, in any tense. A selection of the most common follows below.

a fim de que	in order that	a não ser que	unless
ainda quando / se	even if	ainda que	although
antes que	before	até que	until
(no) caso (que)	in (the) case (that)		
conquanto	although	contanto que	provided that
embora	although	mesmo que	even if
para que	in order that	posto que	although
primeiro que	before	se bem que	although
sem que	without	sob condição que	on condition that

Ele tem de estudar mais a fim de que consiga boas notas. — *He has to study more in order to get good marks.*

Embora tivesses chegado cedo, tudo já tinha sido vendido. — *Although you had arrived early, everything had already been sold.*

Mesmo que não tenhamos dinheiro, vamos jantar fora. — *Even though we haven't any money, let's go and dine out.*

Talvez and *oxalá*

The subjunctive is used after the adverb **talvez** (*perhaps, maybe*) and the interjection **oxalá**, widely used in EP – a wonderful expression coming from Arabic (*God [Allah] willing; hopefully*).

Talvez eles venham mais tarde. — *Perhaps they will come later.*

Oxalá não chova amanhã. — *Let's hope it doesn't rain tomorrow.*

Oxalá can also be used on its own, in response to situations.

Parece que vai ter muito sol para o casamento. Oxalá! — *It looks like it will be very sunny for the wedding. Let's hope so / If only...*

Special expressions

The following expressions also call for the subjunctive:

(por / para…) onde quer que	*wherever*
(a / de…) quem quer que	*whoever*
como quer que	*however*
quando quer que	*whenever*
por mais que	*however much*
por muito(s) que	*however much / many*
por pouco que	*however little*

Por onde quer que se viaje, sempre há turistas!	*Wherever you travel, there are always tourists!*
Por mais que tentes comer menos, nunca terás o corpo da Giselle.	*However much you try to eat less, you'll never have a figure like Giselle's.*

These can be tricky expressions to form correctly, especially to start with, so help yourself take them on board by trying to spot them in your reading, and listen out for them when you are in a Portuguese-speaking country.

Exercises

A Re-work these sentences, starting with **talvez** followed by the present subjunctive.

1 Há mais vinho na cozinha.
2 Estamos ansiosos sem motivo.
3 Dormimos aqui pior do que em casa.
4 Os alunos perdem-se no centro.
5 É preciso contactar a escola.
6 Faço a viagem de barco.
7 Vês melhor sem os óculos de sol!
8 Ele diz mentiras.
9 Queres mais bolo?
10 O rio desce durante a noite.

B Complete the sentences with the correct form of the verbs in brackets, in the present subjunctive.

1 Por muito que …………… (comer), tu nunca ficas gordo.
2 Por mais que …………… (tentar), não conseguem fazer o exercício.
3 Por muito que …………… (dizer), não acreditamos no que diz.
4 Por melhores que …………… (ser) as casas, nunca me quero mudar daqui.

5 Por muito caro que .... (ser), só quer comprar um Audi.

6 Por mais que .... (poupar), nunca têm o suficiente.

7 Por muito longe que .... (ser), vamos de camioneta.

8 Por pouco dinheiro que .... (ter), sempre dá esmolas.

Grammar in context

Why do PAF Port Wines invite you to contact them?

> *Caso não encontre o Vintage ou Colheita*
> *do ano que deseje, CONTACTE-NOS que*
> *a P.A.F. tentará satisfazer o seu pedido.*

44

subjunctive: indefinite and negative antecedents

In this unit you will learn
- using the subjunctive with indefinite or negative antecedents (*someone who can..., nobody who can...*)

Grammar in focus

In relative clauses – those that refer back to the main part of the sentence – introduced by **que**, the subjunctive is used when the antecedent (the person or thing immediately preceding **que**) is not definite or specific. This may be in terms of the article, for example (*the* is definite, *a* is not), or when the antecedent refers to 'someone' or 'anyone'. A negative antecedent, such as *nobody*, also calls for the subjunctive. The easiest way to consider this is to look at some examples.

Procuro alguém que possa trabalhar ao sábados.

I'm looking for someone who can work on Saturdays (i.e. the sort of person who might…).

Queremos um carro que não seja tão pequeno.

We want a car that's not too small (i.e. of the type that is not too small).

Não há ninguém aqui que lhe possa dar esta informação.

There is nobody here who can give you that information.

Ela queria comprar qualquer coisa que servisse de prenda para o primo.

She wanted to buy something that would do as a gift for her cousin.

Look at the differences between the following sentences:

Andamos à procura dum filme que trate da guerra.

We're looking for a film that is about the war.
            SUBJUNCTIVE

Andamos à procura do filme do Spielberg que trata da guerra.

We're looking for Spielberg's film about the war.
            INDICATIVE

Tem sapatos que me sirvam?

Do you have any shoes that fit me?   SUBJUNCTIVE

Tem os sapatos que experimentei ontem?

Do you have the shoes I tried yesterday?   INDICATIVE

Exercise

Ana is looking for people to do various jobs for her. Choose appropriate verbs from the box and form them correctly.

"Procuro alguém que..."

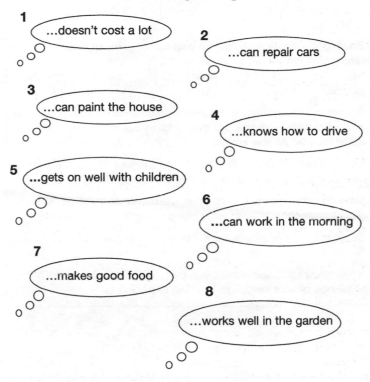

1 ...doesn't cost a lot

2 ...can repair cars

3 ...can paint the house

4 ...knows how to drive

5 ...gets on well with children

6 ...can work in the morning

7 ...makes good food

8 ...works well in the garden

poder pintar a casa	poder trabalhar de manhã
trabalhar bem no jardim	não custar muito
dar-se bem com crianças	fazer boa comida
saber reparar carros	saber conduzir

Language watch 6

In the previous Language watch, we pointed out how you can make your knowledge of other languages work to your benefit to help you guess words in Portuguese. Sometimes, though, this can fall down, as not all words apear to be related! Look at these examples:

English	French	Spanish	Portuguese
tea	té	té	chá
train	train	tren	comboio [BP = trem]
Monday	lundi	lunes	segunda-feira

A word in one language may have a completely different meaning, or an alternative, secondary meaning, in the other. We call these 'false friends' (**falsos amigos**).

for example: assistir = *to attend / be present at*, casualidade = *chance / fortuity*, concurso = *contest / competition*.

Here are some more to look up in the dictionary; you could keep a note of anomalies as you go along.

desgosto   compromisso   bravo   constipado (a great favourite!)

It just shows that sometimes you can't win! Consider it part of the challenge of your language-learning experience.

45

if ... clauses

In this unit you will learn
- how to express possibility in the present
- how to express facts about the past in sentences beginning Se...
- how to talk about the future using Se...

Grammar in focus

Clauses containing the word *if* are known as conditional
sentences, because the word se (*if*) imposes some condition upon
the action. The clauses may state an action which is very likely,
or certain to happen, possibly on a regular basis, in which case
the verb in the clause remains in the indicative mood. The
subjunctive is used in sentences which contain a clause stating
an action which is doubtful to happen, or contrary to fact. The
subjunctive is also used after se when referring to future actions.

Open possibility – present tense

The verb in the 'if' clause goes into the present indicative, while
the main clause may be present, future, or an imperative
(command).

Se me levanto cedo, geralmente faço as compras ao mercado.	*If I get up early, I generally go shopping at the market.*
Se gostas de chocolate, vais adorar estes caramelos.	*If you like chocolate, you'll love these sweets.*
Se não está vendo a televisão, então desligue!	*If you're not watching TV, then switch it off!*

Facts about the past – past tense

When simply stating facts about events which took place in the
past, se can be used with the past tenses.

Se tínhamos tempo, sempre brincávamos antes de voltarmos para casa.	*If we had time, we always used to play before going home.*

Se = whether

When se means *whether*, it is followed by the indicative tenses.
It is used in this sense most often with the verb saber, *to know*.

Ela não sabe se vai à festa.	*She doesn't know if (whether) she's going to the party.*
Não sabíamos se íamos sair de manhã.	*We didn't know if (whether) we were going out in the morning.*

Hypothetical, doubtful actions, contrary to fact – imperfect subjunctive

When expressing 'conditions', i.e. actions subject to doubt, imaginary situations, and actions which may or may not have a solution, the se clause uses the imperfect subjunctive. The verb in the main clause can go in the imperfect indicative or conditional tense. Remember that in colloquial European Portuguese, the conditional can also be replaced by the imperfect tense.

Se eu fosse o meu irmão, compraria (comprava) a moto.	*If I were my brother* [but I'm not], *I would buy the motorbike.*
Se ganhassem muito dinheiro, o que fariam?	*If you won (if you were to win) a lot of money, what would you do?* [an imaginary situation]
Se apanhássemos o comboio [BP = pegássemos o trem], chegávamos mais cedo.	*If we caught the train (were to catch the train), we would arrive earlier.* [a situation which has two possible outcomes; for whatever reason we cannot actually catch the train, or yes, we should catch the train then]

Actions contrary to the statement – past conditionals

When a statement declares something contrary to what actually happened in the past, use the pluperfect subjunctive in the 'if' clause, and the main verb in the imperfect indicative, conditional, or compound tenses of the two.

Se não tivesses gasto tudo, podias ter comprado o livro.	*If you hadn't spent everything, you could have bought the book.*
Se tivessem comprado o bilhete, já eram (seriam) milionários.	*If they had bought the ticket, they would now be millionaires.*
Se tivesse estudado mais, podia ter tido um bom trabalho.	*If I had studied more, I could have had a good job.*

Se and the future

Se is used with the future subjunctive when referring to an action in the future. In English we use the present tense in these situations, so you have to be careful to think about the real meaning and tense of what you want to say in Portuguese. The verbs in the main part of the sentence can go in the present or future indicative, or imperative.

Se ver o teu primo, dou-lhe as notícias, está bem?	*If I see (were to see) your cousin, I'll give him the news, OK?* [Remember that the present tense in Portuguese is often used colloquially in place of the future, hence here **dou**.]
Se tiverem tempo, visitarão o museu dos azulejos.	*If they have the time, they'll visit the tile museum.*
Se fores ao centro, compra um jornal.	*If you go to town (the town centre), buy a paper.*

E se...? = What if...?

You can start a question with **E se...**, when you want to express *What if...?* The verb in the se clause goes into the subjunctive in the relevant tense. This construction is widely used in spoken Portuguese.

E se o João vier mais tarde?	*(And) what if João comes later?*
E se eles não tivessem conseguido entrar?	*(And) what if they hadn't been able to get in?*

Como se... = as if / though...

Use the imperfect or pluperfect subjunctive in this type of construction.

Era como se não conseguisse respirar.	*It was as if I couldn't breathe.*
É como se não tivesse feito nada.	*It's as if / as though he hadn't done anything.*

Exercises

A Complete each sentence by forming the verb correctly, and adding the rest of the sentence from the list of phrses that follows.

1 Se tu não .... (gostar) do Miguel, ...?
2 Se nós .... (chegar) tarde à escola, ...
3 Se você .... (ter) muito dinheiro, ...?
4 Se eles .... (ir) de avião, ...
5 Se tu .... (trazer) o mapa, ...
6 Se a Teresa não .... (convidar) o Roberto, ...
7 Se não .... (ter) tempo hoje, ...
8 Se .... (chover), ...
9 Se tu .... (morar) no Brasil, ...?
10 Se nós .... (reservar) o quarto, ...

a .... o que faria
b .... tudo isto não teria acontecido.
c .... achas que gostarias
d .... porque sempre andas com ele
e .... chegavam mais depressa.
f .... continuamos amanhã.
g .... não tínhamos o problema com alojamento.
h .... os professores ficavam zangados.
i .... não estaríamos perdidos.
j .... eu não vou sair.

B Choose the correct verb from the box to fill the gaps in this dialogue.

A Isabel e a Paula estão a fazer compras (*Isabel and Paula are shopping.*)

Isabel Se não .... nada que fazer, vem comigo às lojas.
Paula Se .... mais cedo, ..., mas já ....
 haver muitas pessoas.
Isabel Não .... nada para o jantar. .... fazer
 compras.
Paula E se .... ao novo supermercado? Se não
 .... tantas pessoas, eu também .... as
 minhas compras.
Isabel Está bem.

Ao supermercado...

Paula Não pensei que .... tão grande! É como se
 .... uma cidade aqui dentro.

Isabel Tens razão. Se .... que havia livros também, ... mais dinheiro. Se ...., trago o meu cartão de crédito.

voltar	houvesse	preciso	fosse	faço
soubesse	deve	fôssemos	tiveres	teria trazido
ia	houver	fosse	tenho	

Grammar in context

How do you win the thousand euros a month for ten years?

46

direct and indirect speech

In this unit you will learn
• how to convert direct to
  indirect speech in
  Portuguese: which verbs,
  tenses, pronouns and
  possessives to use

Grammar in focus

Direct speech is where the exact words of the speaker are recorded, in whatever tense that may be, with the punctuation of speech marks to indicate that this is a replica of the original statement. Indirect speech, on the other hand, is often referred to as 'reported speech', as it is a report of what was said, and is preceded by expressions such as: *She said that...*, *They suggested that...* . It is important when moving from direct to indirect speech to take into account tenses, pronouns, prepositions and adverbs of place and time, as all of these may need to change.

Punctuation

Direct speech is usually indicated by speech marks (quotation marks) around the words spoken, with question marks where appropriate. Indirect speech does not share these features.

Verbs of speech

Both types of speech make use of verbs such as to say, to ask, to suggest, to reply, etc., but in indirect speech they are followed by the word *that* (**que**), although 'that' is not always expressed in English.

Tenses and moods

Normal rules for tense construction apply in direct speech; in indirect, the verb following the **que** changes tense, as too may other verbs within the statement, mostly in ways they would do in English (see the examples below). With verbs of suggesting, wishing, etc., the subjunctive tense sequence rules still apply.

Pronouns and possessives

Direct speech is carried out in the first and second person; indirect can be reported in all three (*I said that*, *you suggested that*, *he replied that...*). Possessives will change, e.g. *I'm taking my hat* → *You said that you were taking your hat*.

Demonstratives

The words for 'this' in direct speech may become 'that' in indirect.

Adverbs of place

Words expressing proximity, such as *here*, *in this place*, etc., become *there* and *in that place* in indirect speech.

Adverbs of time

Time references also change – see the table below for some examples.

The following comparison may help to illustrate some of the changes between the two forms of speech.

	Direct speech	Indirect speech
Punctuation	Speech marks or lines, question marks, exclamation marks	None
Verbs of speech	Verbs such as: **contar, dizer, responder, sugerir, saber** etc.	Same range of verbs, followed by **que, se** or **para**
Tense / mood	present indicative	imperfect indicative
	preterite	pluperfect
	future	conditional
	present subjunctive	imperfect subjunctive
	imperfect subj.	imperfect subj.
	future subjunctive	imperfect subj.
	imperative	imperfect subj. *or* infinitive
Pronouns / possessives	Mostly first and second person	Changes may occur to all
Demonstratives	**este, esse** etc.	**aquele,** etc.
	isto, isso	**aquilo**
Adverbs of place	**aqui**	**ali**
	cá	**lá**
	neste lugar, etc.	**naquele lugar,** etc.
Adverbs of time	**ontem**	**no dia anterior**
	hoje	**nesse dia / naquele dia**
	amanhã	**no dia seguinte**
	agora	**naquele momento**
	no próximo mês	**no mês seguinte**

Let's consider some examples to see how it works in practice.

«Vou a casa da minha tia», disse a Beatrice.	*'I'm going to my aunt's house', said Beatrice.*
A Beatrice disse que ia a casa da tia (dela).	*Beatrice said that she was going to her aunt's house.*
«A festa foi boa; deram-me um grande bolo», contou o Luís.	*'The party was good; they gave me a huge cake', Luis recounted (said).*
Luís contou que a festa tinha sido boa, e que lhe tinham dado um grande bolo.	*Luis said that the party had been good and that they had given him a huge cake.*

«Põe mais açúcar no café!», pediu-me a minha mãe.

'Put more sugar in the coffee', my mother asked me.

A minha mãe pediu-me que pusesse mais açúcar no café / pediu-me para pôr ...

My mother asked me to put more sugar in the coffee.

«Na semana passada os meus primos passaram dois dias cá em casa», disse a Paula.

'Last week my cousins spent two days here at home,' said Paula.

A Paula disse que na semana anterior, os primos (dela) tinham passado dois dias lá em casa dela.

Paula said that in the previous week, her cousins had spent two days there at her home.

«Quem quer ir à praia?» perguntou.

'Who wants to go to the beach?' she asked.

Perguntou quem queria ir à praia.

She asked who wanted to go to the beach.

This is not the easiest part of Portuguese grammar to master quickly, so don't worry if it takes a while to sort out the sequences. Reported speech often occurs in magazine articles, so you may be able to familiarize yourself with the way the sentences are written. Some articles may be in the form of an interview with a famous person, with answers in direct speech. Why not try working out how to re-write them as indirect speech? You also hear reported speech on TV programmes, especially the news – a good excuse to watch television when you are in a Portuguese-speaking country. The only problem is that news presenters do speak very quickly, so don't be disheartened if you catch very little at first. Be persistent, and it will eventually pay off!

Exercise

Read this interview (adapted from *TV Mais* magazine) with Ediberto Lima, TV producer, then see if you can report what he said. Write seven sentences.

Quais são os seus programas favoritos?
Gosto mais dos meus próprios programas.

Que programa nunca perde?
O Telejornal, porque tenho de saber as notícias.

Qual é, para si, o melhor apresentador de televisão?
Para mim, cá em Portugal, tem de ser Jorge Gabriel.

Vê futebol na televisão?
Sempre. Ontem, por exemplo, vi um jogo muito bom.

O que não suporta ver na televisão?
Os congressos dos partidos políticos. Amanhã, se houver este programa, desligo a televisão.

Qual é, na sua opinião, o melhor filme de sempre?
Na minha opinião, é, sem dúvida, A Corda, de Alfred Hitchcock.

O *Big Show SIC* vai continuar?
Se é para o bem de todos e felicidade geral da nação, digo ao povo que sim!

O Ediberto disse...

Grammar in context

'Quote, Unquote'

Here are some newspaper quotes from a variety of people. See if you can discover who (a–f) said what...

1
> *'Os contratos matrimoniais deveriam ser redigidos como a licença para cão e ser renovados todos os anos.'*

(on the renewal of wedding vows)

2
> *'Se eu soubesse qual era a situação do Benfica não me tinha candidatado.'*

(on taking over at troubled football club Benfica)

3
> *'A minha carreira foi sempre completamente transparente. Tudo o que fiz é visível para toda a gente. Mesmo o futebol. É sangue, suor e lágrimas no campo.'*

(on how he gained so much wealth in so little time)

4

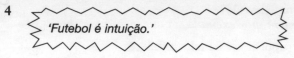

'*Futebol é intuição.*'

(on… football!)

5

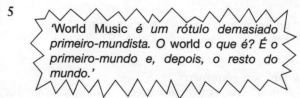

'World Music *é um rótulo demasiado primeiro-mundista. O world o que é? É o primeiro-mundo e, depois, o resto do mundo.*'

(on the concept of 'world music')

6

'*Foi mais simples do que fazer uma tatuagem.*'

(on being present at his son's birth)

a Manuel Vilarinho, President of 'The Reds' football club
b Silvio Berlusconi
c Liam Gallagher (Oasis)
d Rod Stewart
e Brazilian singer Marisa Monte
f Footballer Ronaldo

European and Brazilian Portuguese: some differences in vocabulary

European	Brazilian	English
alcatifa	tapete	*carpet, rug*
ananás	abacaxí	*pineapple*
apanhar	pegar	*to catch*
aquecer	esquentar	*to heat, warm*
autocarro	ônibus	*bus*
bica/café	cafezinho	*small coffee*
bicha	fila	*queue*
bolacha	biscoito	*biscuit*
boléia	carona	*lift* (in a car, etc.)
camioneta	ônibus de luxo	*coach*
camisola	malha	*sweater*
cão	cachorro	*dog*
carro eléctrico	bonde	*tram*
casa de banho	banheiro	*bathroom*
chávena	xícara	*cup*
comboio	trem	*train*
desporto	esporte	*sport*
disparate	besteira	*nonsense*
ementa / lista	cardápio	*menu*
empregado	garçom	*waiter*
esquadra	delegacia	*police station*
fato	terno	*suit*
fiambre	presunto	*boiled ham*
frigorífico	geladeira	*fridge*
gelado	sorvete	*ice-cream*
imperial	chope	*draught lager*
mamã	mamãe	*Mum, mummy*

European	Brazilian	English
marcar o número	discar	*to dial* (phone)
montra	vitrine	*shop window*
mulher-a-dias	faxineira	*cleaning lady*
peão	pedestre	*pedestrian*
pequeno almoço	café da manhã	*breakfast*
peúgas	meias	*socks*
prenda	presente	*gift*
rapariga	moça	*girl*
rebuçado	bala	*sweet*
sumo	suco	*fruit juice*
talho	açougue	*butcher's*
tenda	barraca	*tent*
ver	enxergar	*to see (notice)*
verniz	esmalte	*nail varnish*

Regular verbs

Present indicative			Present subjunctive			Imperfect indicative		
-ar	-er	-ir	-ar	-er	-ir	-ar	-er	-ir
-o	-o	-o	-e	-a	-a	-ava	-ia	-ia
-as	-es	-es	-es	-as	-as	-avas	-ias	-ias
-a	-e	-e	-e	-a	-a	-ava	-ia	-ia
-amos	-emos	-imos	-emos	-amos	-amos	-ávamos	-íamos	-íamos
-ais	-eis	-is	-eis	-ais	-ais	-áveis	-íeis	-íeis
-am	-em	-em	-em	-am	-am	-avam	-iam	-iam

Preterite			Pluperfect			Imperfect subjunctive		
-ar	-er	-ir	-ar	-er	-ir	-ar	-er	-ir
-ei	-i	-i	-ara	-era	-ira	-asse	-esse	-isse
-aste	-este	-iste	-aras	-eras	-iras	-asses	-esses	-isses
-ou	-eu	-iu	-ara	-era	-ira	-asse	-esse	-isse
-ámos	-emos	-imos	-áramos	-éramos	-íramos	-ássemos	-êssemos	-íssemos
-astes	-estes	-istes	-áreis	-éreis	-íreis	-ásseis	-êsseis	-ísseis
-aram	-eram	-iram	-aram	-eram	-iram	-assem	-essem	-issem

Future subjunctive			Future indicative			Conditional		
-ar	-er	-ir	-ar	-er	-ir	-ar	-er	-ir
-ar	-er	-ir	-ei	-ei	-ei	-ia	-ia	-ia
-ares	-eres	-ires	-ás	-ás	-ás	-ias	-ias	-ias
-ar	-er	-ir	-á	-á	-á	-ia	-ia	-ia
-armos	-ermos	-irmos	-emos	-emos	-emos	-íamos	-íamos	-íamos
-ardes	-erdes	-irdes	-eis	-eis	-eis	-íeis	-íeis	-íeis
-arem	-erem	-irem	-ão	-ão	-ão	-iam	-iam	-iam

Imperative			Past participle			Gerund		
-ar	-er	-ir	-ar	-er	-ir	-er	-er	-ir
–	–	–						
-a	-e	-e						
(-e)	(-a)	(-a)	-ado	-ido	-ido	-ando	-endo	-indo
(-emos)	(-amos)	(-amos)						
-ai	-ei	-i						
(-em)	(-am)	(-am)						

Irregular verbs

	Present indicative	Present subjunctive	Imperfect indicative	Preterite PAST	Pluperfect
crer (*to believe*)	creio crês crê cremos credes crêem	creia creias creia creiamos creiais creiam	regular	regular	regular
dar (*to give*)	dou dás dá damos dais dão	dê dês dê dêmos deis dêem	regular	dei deste deu demos destes deram	dera deras dera déramos déreis deram
dizer (*to say*)	digo dizes diz dizemos dizeis dizem	diga digas diga digamos digais digam	regular	disse disseste disse dissemos dissestes disseram	dissera disseras dissera disséramos disséreis disseram
estar (*to be*)	estou estás está estamos estais estão	esteja estejas esteja estejamos estejais estejam	regular	estive estiveste esteve estivemos estivestes estiveram	estivera estiveras estivera estivéramos estivéreis estiveram
fazer (*to do, make*)	faço fazes faz fazemos fazeis fazem	faça faças faça façamos façais façam	regular	fiz fizeste fez fizemos fizestes fizeram	fizera fizeras fizera fizéramos fizéreis fizeram
haver (*to have*)	hei hás há havemos haveis hão	haja hajas haja hajamos hajais hajam	regular	houve houveste houve houvemos houvestes houveram	houvera houveras houvera houvéramos houvéreis houveram
ir (*to go*)	vou vais vai vamos ides vão	vá vás vá vamos vades vão	regular (ia, *etc.*)	fui went foste foi went fomos fostes foram	fora foras fora fôramos fôreis foram

Imperfect subjunctive	Future subjunctive	Future indicative	Conditional	Imperative	Past participle	Gerund
regular	*regular*	*regular*	*regular*	– crê (creia) (creiamos) crede (creiam)	crido	crendo
desse desses desse déssemos désseis dessem	der deres der dermos derdes derem	*regular*	*regular*	– dá (dê) (dêmos) dai (dêem)	dado	dando
dissesse dissesses dissesse disséssemos dissésseis dissessem	disser disseres disser dissermos disserdes disserem	direi dirás dirá diremos direis dirão	diria dirias diria diríamos diríeis diriam	– diz(e) (diga) (digamos) dizei (digam)	dito	dizendo
estivesse estivesses estivesse estivéssemos estivésseis estivessem	estiver estiveres estiver estivermos estiverdes estiverem	*regular*	*regular*	– está (esteja) (estejamos) estai (estejam)	estado	estando
fizesse fizesses fizesse fizéssemos fizésseis fizessem	fizer fizeres fizer fizermos fizerdes fizerem	farei farás fará faremos fareis farão	faria farias faria faríamos faríeis fariam	– faz(e) (faça) (façamos) fazei (façam)	feito	fazendo
houvesse houvesses houvesse houvéssemos houvésseis houvessem	houver houveres houver houvermos houverdes houverem	*regular*	*regular*	– há (haja) (hajamos) havei (hajam)	havido	havendo
fosse fosses fosse fôssemos fôsseis fossem	for fores for formos fordes forem	*regular*	*regular*	– vai (vá) (vamos) ide (vão)	ido	indo

	Present indicative	Present subjunctive	Imperfect indicative	Preterite	Pluperfect
ler (*to read*)	leio lês lê lemos ledes lêem	leia leias leia leiamos leiais leiam	*regular*	*regular*	*regular*
medir (*to measure*)	meço medes mede medimos medis medem	meça meças meça meçamos meçais meçam	*regular*	*regular*	*regular*
ouvir (*to hear*)	ouço ouves ouve ouvimos ouvis ouvem	ouça ouças ouça ouçamos ouçais ouçam	*regular*	*regular*	*regular*
pedir (*to ask for*)	peço pedes pede pedimos pedis pedem	peça peças peça peçamos peçais peçam	*regular*	*regular*	*regular*
perder (*to lose*)	perco perdes perde perdemos perdeis perdem	perca percas perca percamos percais percam	*regular*	*regular*	*regular*
poder (*can, may, to be able*)	posso podes pode podemos podeis podem	possa possas possa possamos possais possam	*regular*	pude pudeste pôde pudemos pudestes puderam	pudera puderas pudera pudéramos pudéreis puderam
pôr (*to put*)	ponho pões põe pomos pondes põem	ponha ponhas ponha ponhamos ponhais ponham	punha punhas punha púnhamos púnheis punham	pus puseste pôs pusemos pusestes puseram	pusera puseras pusera puséramos puséreis puseram

Imperfect subjunctive	Future subjunctive	Future indicative	Conditional	Imperative	Past participle	Gerund
regular	*regular*	*regular*	*regular*	– lê (leia) (leiamos) lede (leiam)	lido	lendo
regular	*regular*	*regular*	*regular*	– mede (meça) (meçamos) medi (meçam)	medido	medindo
regular	*regular*	*regular*	*regular*	– ouve (ouça) (ouçamos) ouvi (ouçam)	ouvido	ouvindo
regular	*regular*	*regular*	*regular*	– pede (peça) (peçamos) pedi (peçam)	pedido	pedindo
regular	*regular*	*regular*	*regular*	– perde (perca) (percamos) perdei (percam)	perdido	perdendo
pudesse pudesses pudesse pudéssemos pudésseis pudessem	puder puderes puder pudermos puderdes puderem	*regular*	*regular*	– pode (possa) (possamos) podei (possam)	podido	podendo
pusesse pusesses pusesse puséssemos pusésseis pusessem	puser puseres puser pusermos puserdes puserem	*regular*	*regular*	– põe (ponha) (ponhamos) ponde (ponham)	posto	pondo

	Present indicative	Present subjunctive	Imperfect indicative	Preterite	Pluperfect
querer (*to want*)	quero queres quer queremos quereis querem	queira queiras queira queiramos querais queiram	*regular*	quis quiseste quis quisemos quisestes quiseram	quisera quiseras quisera quiséramos quiséreis quiseram
rir (*to laugh*)	rio ris ri rimos rides riem	ria rias ria riamos riais riam	*regular*	*regular*	*regular*
saber (*to know, know how to*)	sei sabes sabe sabemos sabeis sabem	saiba saibas saiba saibamos saibais saibam	*regular*	soube soubeste soube soubemos soubestes souberam	soubera souberas soubera soubéramos soubéreis souberam
ser (*to be*)	sou és é somos sois são	seja sejas seja sejamos sejais sejam	era eras era éramos éreis eram	fui WAS foste foi WAS fomos WERE fostes foram WERE	fora foras fora fôramos fôreis foram
ter (*to have*)	tenho tens tem temos tendes têm	tenha tenhas tenha tenhamos tenhais tenham	tinha tinhas tinha tínhamos tínheis tinham	tive tiveste teve tivemos tivestes tiveram	tivera tiveras tivera tivéramos tivéreis tiveram
trazer (*to bring*)	trago trazes traz trazemos trazeis trazem	traga tragas traga tragamos tragais tragam	*regular*	trouxe trouxeste trouxe trouxemos trouxestes trouxeram	trouxera trouxeras trouxera trouxéramos trouxéreis trouxeram
valer (*to be worth*)	valho vales vale valemos valeis valem	valha valhas valha valhamos valhais valham	*regular*	*regular*	*regular*

Imperfect subjunctive	Future subjunctive	Future indicative	Conditional	Imperative	Past participle	Gerund
quisesse quisesses quisesse quiséssemos quisésseis quisessem	quiser quiseres quiser quisermos quiserdes quiserem	*regular*	*regular*	– quer(e) (queira) (queiramos) querei (queiram)	querido	querendo
regular	*regular*	*regular*	*regular*	– ri (ria) (riamos) ride (riam)	rido	rindo
soubesse soubesses soubesse soubéssemos soubésseis soubessem	souber souberes souber soubermos souberdes souberem	*regular*	*regular*	– sabe (saiba) (saibamos) sabei (saibam)	sabido	sabendo
fosse fosses fosse fôssemos fôsseis fossem	for fores for formos fordes forem	*regular*	*regular*	– sê (seja) (sejamos) sede (sejam)	sido	sendo
tivesse tivesses tivesse tivéssemos tivésseis tivessem	tiver tiveres tiver tivermos tiverdes tiverem	*regular*	*regular*	– tem (tenha) (tenhamos) tende (tenham)	tido	tendo
trouxesse trouxesses trouxesse trouxéssemos trouxésseis trouxessem	trouxer trouxeres trouxer trouxermos trouxerdes trouxerem	trarei trarás trará traremos trareis trarão	traria trarias traria traríamos traríeis trariam	– traz(e) (traga) (tragamos) trazei (tragam)	trazido	trazendo
regular	*regular*	*regular*	*regular*	– vale (valha) (valhamos) valei (valham)	valido	valendo

	Present indicative	Present subjunctive	Imperfect indicative	Preterite	Pluperfect
ver (*to see*)	vejo	veja		vi	vira
	vês	vejas		viste	viras
	vê	veja	*regular*	viu	vira
	vemos	vejamos		vimos	víramos
	vedes	vejais		vistes	víreis
	vêem	vejam		viram	viram
vir (*to come*)	venho	venha	vinha	vim	viera
	vens	venhas	vinhas	vieste	vieras
	vem	venha	vinha	veio	viera
	vimos	venhamos	vínhamos	viemos	viéramos
	vindes	venhais	vínheis	viestes	viéreis
	vêm	venham	vinham	vieram	vieram

Imperfect subjunctive	Future subjunctive	Future indicative	Conditional	Imperative	Past participle	Gerund
visse	vir			–		
visses	vires			vê		
visse	vir	*regular*	*regular*	(veja)	visto	vendo
víssemos	virmos			(vejamos)		
vísseis	virdes			vede		
vissem	virem			(vejam)		
viesse	vier			–		
viesses	vieres			vem		
viesse	vier	*regular*	*regular*	(venha)	vindo	vindo
viéssemos	viermos			(venhamos)		
viésseis	vierdes			vinde		
viessem	vierem			(venham)		

taking it further

There follows a selection of information on further reading, websites, and other useful sources for learning Portuguese.

Reading

História da Língua portuguesa, Paul Teyssier, Sá da Costa, 1990

The Romance languages, Martin Harris and Nigel Vincent (Routledge, 1997)

The Loom of Language, Frederick Bodmer (Allen & Unwin, 1946)

Dicionário Editora da língua portuguesa, a good monolingual dictionary (new edn. 1994)

Oxford–Duden pictorial dictionary, detailed visual vocabulary (1992)

Michaelis dicionário práctico, bilingual (English/Portuguese, both directions)

Collins Portuguese dictionaries, various sizes.

Learning

There is a BBC series, *Discovering Portuguese*, which is often repeated, and worth video-taping. It comprises six programmes of background scenes of Portugal, and language, although some parts need updating. A new series, *Talk Portuguese*, was broadcast from 2003. Satellite TV, if you have access to it, will be able to reach Portuguese TV; there is an international channel called RTPi.

There are online courses, such as that offered by the University of Glasgow (UK), called *De tudo um pouco*.

Dicionário Universal da língua portuguesa is a CD-ROM version of a Portuguese dictionary (Texto Editora). Visit their website at: http://www.priberam.pt/DLPO/

Various CD-ROMs for learning Portuguese are now available from good bookstores.

Enrol on language courses at your local college / language school. Try to speak with Portuguese people when you are in Portugal – they will be grateful you have made an effort, and will encourage your attempts.

Places

Camões Institute, R. Rodrigues Sampaio 113, 1150-279 Lisboa. Tel: 213-109-100 (see below for website)

Coordination of Portuguese Language Centres world-wide, Centro Coordenador dos Centros de Língua Portuguesa, Campo Grande 56, r/c, 1700-078 Lisboa. Tel: 217-956-113

Websites

There are many sites and materials in both English and Portuguese. Here are just a few ideas:

Camões Institute – language and cultural information http://www.instituto-camoes.pt
Comunidade de Países de Língua Portuguesa – Portuguese-speaking communities: http://www.cplp.org
Portugal and the Portuguese language – http://www.public.iastate.edu/~pedro/pt_connect.html
The Human Languages Page – materials, interesting links, institutions and information in the language of your choice: http://www.june29.com
King's College, London – Dept. of Portuguese and Brazilian studies, various links: http://www.kcl.ac.uk/depsta/humanities/pobrst/kclhp.htm
Língua Portuguesa – Key this into search motor Altavista, and you should link to many more sites.
Grant & Cutler – stockists of Portuguese books in the UK: http://www.grant-c.demon.co.uk
For all sorts of information: http://www.portugal-info.net
Portuguese National Library: http://www.bn.pt/
Publishers Lidel–Edições Técnicas Lda: http://www.lidel.pt
Publishers Porto Editora: http://www.portoeditora.pt
Portuguese bookshop: http://www.mediabooks.com

Many newspapers are available online; here is a selection:
http://www.expresso.pt   http://www.oindependente.pt
   http://jn.sapo.pt/   http://dn.sap.pt/   http://www.publico.pt
   http://www.euronoticias.pt

Radio and TV stations can also be found online; here are some:
   http://www.rdp.pt   http://www.radiocomercial.iol.pt/
   http://www.rtp.pt

News site: http://www.diariodigital.pt/

Online magazine for women:
   http://www.mulherportuguesa.com/

Cinema: http://www.7arte.net

Unit 2

A 1 o (*book*) 2 o (*gentleman*) 3 a (*table*) 4 o (*country*) 5 a (*mother*) 6 o (*restaurant*) 7 a (*information*) 8 a (*garage*) 9 o (*coffee / café*) 10 a (*city*)

B

J	A	B	C	T	D	E	F	G	P
O	A	H	I	Ú	J	K	L	M	A
V	N	R	O	M	P	Q	R	S	Í
E	T	A	D	E	U	T	I	O	S
N	V	P	X	I	Y	Z	B	D	E
S	F	A	H	S	N	J	L	N	S
P	R	Z	T	V	X	S	Z	C	E
S	I	E	N	Ú	T	O	R	T	V
X	Z	S	D	F	H	Ã	J	L	N
C	A	S	A	S	T	M	V	X	Z

C 1 o 2 uma 3 X 4 a 5 X 6 X 7 o 8 os

Grammar in context 1 chicken (**frango**), newspaper (**jornal**), dictionary (**dicionário**) 2 ½ kilo 3 um pão

Unit 3

A 1 pequeno 2 bonita 3 tristes 4 felizes 5 feroz 6 alta

B 1A americanos 2D branco 3A vermelha 4D verdes 5A alemã 6D castanhos 7A azuis 8D espanhóis 9A inglês 10D brasileira

Grammar in context a) especial, pequeno (almoço), situado, invejável, turística, tradicional, magnífica, directo, fácil, aquecida b) boas-vindas, circundantes, populares, válidos, mencionados

Unit 4

A 1 extremamente 2 temporariamente 3 finalmente 4 bem 5 rapidamente 6 realmente 7 silenciosamente 8 secretamente 9 francamente 10 exactamente [BP = exatamente]

B 1 c 2 d 3 b 4 f 5 a 6 e

Unit 5

A 1 maior 2 mais caro 3 tão fria 4 menos rapidamente 5 menos de

B 1 T 2 T 3 F 4 F 5 T 6 F

C 1 tardíssimo 2 gordíssima 3 pesadíssimas 4 gravíssimo 5 dificílimo 6 caríssimos

Grammar in context Because it's tastier in Bahia.

Unit 6

A 1 estas 2 esse 3 aquela 4 esses 5 esta 6 aqueles 7 este 8 essas 9 aquele 10 estes

B 1 O que é isto? 2 Isso é um livro. 3 estas senhoras aqui 4 aquele chapéu ali 5 That is a dictionary. 6 These are glasses ('this thing here – they're glasses'). 7 That cake is made of almond. 8 Salvador and Campinas are cities in Brazil; the latter is in the south, the former in the north.

Grammar in context aquela blusa (*that blouse*), esta (*this one*), estas (*these*), essa (*that one*), aquilo (*that one*) x 2, esta blusa (*this blouse*)

Unit 7

A 1 a minha 2 os meus 3 o teu 4 os teus 5 a sua 6 as suas 7 o nosso 8 os nossos 9 a vossa 10 as vossas

B 1 b 2 c 3 b 4 c 5 a 6 b

Grammar in context 1 Ana Maria 2 Joana's father 3 Nuno's brother and sister-in-law 4 Joana's grandmother 5 Joana's brother-in-law (Nuno's brother)

Unit 8

A 1 c 2 h 3 e 4 a 5 j 6 f 7 b 8 g 9 d 10 i

B 1 cujas casas são brancas 2 cujos resultados são os melhores 3 cuja roupa é Nike 4 cuja capa é de couro 5 cujo chapéu é azul

Grammar in context onde que que onde

Unit 9

A 1 debaixo da árvore 2 no rio 3 em cima duma ponte 4 atrás / detrás dum balde 5 em frente das flores 6 entre a pá e a forquilha 7 dentro do barril 8 longe do lago

B 1 ao 2 às 3 para 4 da 5 de 6 na 7 no 8 para 9 por 10 pelas

Grammar in context Incorrect statements are: 3, 5, 6

Unit 10

A 1 para 2 por 3 para 4 para 5 por 6 por 7 por 8 para 9 para 10 para

B 1 correct 2 correct 3 incorrect 4 correct 5 incorrect 6 incorrect 7 correct 8 incorrect 9 correct 10 correct

Unit 11

A 1 quem 2 onde 3 quando 4 quantos 5 como 6 quantas 7 porque 8 quando 9 como 10 quem

B 1 Nunca... 2 Ninguém... 3 Nunca... 4 Não... nada 5 Não, não... 6 Não há... nenhuma parte... 7 Não tenho nenhuma... 8 Não gostam nem do filme, nem da música 9 Não sabe nada... 10 Ninguém...

Grammar in context 1. Ninguém (neg.) 2. Porquê? / de quê? (interrog.) 3. Que linda! (exclam.)

Unit 12

A

G	A	I	R	A	T	A	P	A	S
A	Z	A	B	C	O	E	F	A	H
R	E	K	L	M	Ã	V	P	I	A
R	L	U	V	W	D	E	Z	R	D
A	E	M	E	S	I	N	H	A	A
F	B	N	O	P	T	D	S	R	L
Ã	W	X	Y	Z	N	E	C	V	E
O	Ã	T	A	G	E	D	M	I	P
P	Q	R	S	T	L	O	W	L	A
F	I	G	U	E	I	R	A	H	P

B 1 casinha / casarão 2 infeliz / felizmente 3 descontente 4 carta / cartão 5 prever / rever 6 amoral 7 gatinho / gatão 8 compor / descompor 9 refazer / perfazer / desfazer 10 perfeito

Grammar in context 1 Little port (o porto) 2 diabinho (*little devil*), anjinho (*little angel*)

Unit 13

A toda a loja todos os alunos todas as pessoas todo este mês a primavera toda fomos nós todos toda torcida ambas casas ambos partiram ambas aquelas cada uma cada 40 minutos cada cinco semanas

B 1 The hat is all dirty. 2 Everyone wanted to go to the theatre. 3 We spend the whole summer on the beach. 4 I want to buy everything (it all). 5 There is a boat every three days. 6 That's 6 Euros 75 in all. 7 I'm going to do everything possible to improve. 8 All the museums are closed today. 9 Both these houses are pretty. 10 Everyone (every person) has a ticket.

C 1 every weekend 2 all kinds 3 both (two) 4 he visits all the parts of the Algarve 5 it's all very pretty

Grammar in context 1 housewives 2 **a** every day **b** no, it's made on the spot.

Unit 14

A 1 catorze (quatorze) 2 trinta e seis 3 setenta e oito 4 cento e vinte e um 5 cento e noventa e nove 6 quatrocentos e cinquenta 7 mil e sessenta e cinco 8 mil, trezentos e quarenta e quatro 9 três mil e seiscentos 10 vinte e seis mil, oitocentos e quarenta e dois 11 duzentos e quarenta e seis mil 12 um milhão, quinhentos e trinta e dois mil, novecentos e doze

B 134: cento e trinta e quatro 25: vinte e cinco 521: quinhentos e vinte e um 122: cento e vinte e dois 1.018: mil e dezoito 4.222: quatro mil, duzentos e vinte e dois 912: novecentos e doze

C 1 b 2 a 3 c 4 b 5 a 6 c

Grammar in context 1 noventa e um euros 2 vinte e seis 3 vinte por cento 4 dezoito euros e vinte 5 vinte e cinco euros e trinta e cinco 6 *Super Interessante*

Unit 15

A 1 cento e vinte e cinco mais setenta e cinco são duzentos 2 oitenta e cinco menos trinta e cinco dão cinquenta 3 dezasseis multiplicado por quatro são sessenta e quatro 4 mil dividido por dez dá cem 5 dois quintos 6 três décimos 7 cinco oitavos 8 dezassete vírgula dois 9 dois vírgula cinco seis 10 treze metros quadrados

B Quarto 1: 8 m 6 m 48 m² 28 m Quarto 2: 6 m 5 m 30 m² 22 m Cozinha: 7 m 4 m 28 m² 22 m Apt. total: 19 m 15 m 285 m² 68 m

Unit 16

A 1 quinta-feira 2 Janeiro 3 Verão 4 Setembro 5 terça 6 domingo 7 Julho The missing season is **Inverno** (*winter*).

B 1 a 10 2 8 3 sexta-feira 4 16 5 13, 25 6 a Páscoa 7 segunda 8 sábado

C 1 às oito 2 entre as três e as seis / das três (até) às seis 3 São seis e quarenta / sete menos vinte / vinte para as sete. 4 Eram quatro e dez. 5 às nove e cinquenta e cinco 6 a partir das sete e meia

Grammar in context 1 10a.m.–7p.m. 2 7p.m. 3 no (unless it's a national holiday – **feriado**)

Unit 17

A 1 vendo-os 2 comprámo-la 3 deu-lhe 4 devolvê-los 5 viu-nos 6 emprestas-lhe 7 enviaram-nos 8 vê-o 9 visitamos-te 10 diz-lhes

B 1 yes 2 yes 3 no 4 yes 5 no 6 no 7 yes 8 yes 9 no 10 yes

C 1 o 2 lhe 3 lhe 4 connosco 5 lo 6 mim 7 consigo 8 nos 9 me 10 lho

Grammar in context Because you like animals, help us to defend them!

Unit 18

A 1 c 2 f 3 a 4 e 5 d 6 b

B 1 In winter it gets dark earlier. 2 Não me apetece ir à festa. 3 What do you think? 4 Não nos interessa o dinheiro. 5 I miss my girlfriend. 6 Há um hospital aqui? 7 The book is about a tragedy. 8 Quanto custa o chapéu?

Grammar in context all week

Unit 19

A 1 c 2 d 3 a 4 f 5 b 6 e 7 h 8 g

B 1 b 2 f 3 a / d / e 4 a / d / e 5 g / h 6 c 7 a / d / e 8 g / h

Grammar in context 1 receiving / welcoming well 2 serving well

Unit 20

A 1 estudo 2 compramos 3 bebes 4 responde 5 abre 6 subis 7 limpam 8 partem 9 escuta 10 come

B 1 fecham 2 bebemos 3 serve 4 moro 5 chove 6 abrem 7 jogas 8 compreendeis 9 parte 10 lavam

Grammar in context 1 historical, rural, commercial 2 granite 3 Vinho Verde 4 cobre, enriquece, sabe, serve-se

Unit 21

A 1 receio 2 receia 3 divertes 4 divertis 5 sentir 6 sentimos 7 durmo 8 dormem 9 sobes 10 subimos 11 odiar 12 odeia

B **1** Receias o exame? **2** Odiamos o Inverno. **3** Não consigo comer mais. **4** Mente. **5** Repetis a frase. **6** Cobrem a criança. **7** Descubro o segredo. **8** Sobes?

Grammar in context **1** the true charm of the Minho **2** in their park in Vilar de Mouros

Unit 22

A **1** a **2** c **3** b **4** a **5** c **6** b **7** a **8** b **9** a **10** c

B **1** e **2** a **3** h **4** b **5** j **6** g **7** i **8** c **9** d **10** f

Grammar in context Pay for one, take two (Buy one, get one free)

Unit 23

A **1** sento-me **2** lavas-te **3** se deita **4** levantamo-nos **5** se chama **6** corto-me **7** vêem-se **8** vestes-te **9** ela não se sente bem **10** esquecem-se

B **1** te levantas **2** senta-se **3** esqueci-me **4** veste-se **5** nos encontramos **6** deitam-se **7** me vesti **8** se chama **9** se lembra **10** se lavaram

Unit 24

A **1** i [a] **2** f [a] **3** a [em] **4** c [por] **5** h [com] **6** g [para] **7** k [a] **8** j [de] **9** e [em] **10** l [por] **11** b [com] **12** d [para]

B **1** A Ana aprendia a conduzir / dirigir. **2** Faz (etc.) bem em reclamar; é muito / demasiado caro. **3** Esta situação serve para ilustrar as dificuldades de viver num país estrangeiro. **4** A luta levou-me a ficar em casa durante duas semanas. **5** Os homens foram prevenidos de se aproximar. **6** O meu irmão sempre suspirava por viajar pelo mundo.

Grammar in context It served to wipe out the memory of the game against Finland.

Unit 25

A The correct order in the preterite should be (original number in brackets): (**11**) saí (**6**) apanhei [BP = peguei] (**1**) cheguei (**12**) comprei (**7**) comprei (**2**) bebi (**13**) encontrei (**8**) marcou (**3**) comi (**14**) fui (**9**) cometeu (**15**) expulsou (**4**) transformou (**10**) marcou (**5**) ganhou (**16**) estiveram

B 1 encontraram 2 pagaste 3 abriram 4 falei 5 compraram 6 falámos 7 tocou 8 leu

Grammar in context Arrived Tuesday / Wed visited a Vinho Verde (wine) estate / husband went to Pinhão on historical train / stayed in small hotel in centre of Vila Real / she liked the sweet things

Unit 26

A 1 Vivia no campo. 2 Jogava futebol todos os dias. 3 Não frequentava a escola muito. 4 Lia no jardim. 5 Ajudava em casa 6 Saía com amigos. 7 Fazia bolos com a mãe. 8 Ia à igreja aos domingos.

B 1 podia 2 queríamos 3 diziam 4 gostavas 5 ia 6 tinha 7 eram 8 estudavas/ lavávamos 9 costumavam 10 comia

Grammar in context era, ser, *to be* havia, haver, *to have* olhava, olhar, *to look* pensava, pensar, *to think* conseguia, conseguir, *to manage to* podiam, poder, *to be able* tinha, ter, *to have*

Unit 27

A 1 h 2 e 3 a 4 j 5 b 6 i 7 d 8 c 9 g 10 f

B 1 correct 2 correct 3 incorrect: fui 4 incorrect: vestia-se *or* estava vestido 5 correct 6 incorrect: saía 7 correct 8 incorrect: atendi 9 incorrect: pintou 10 correct

C vendi vendia partem partiam compras compraste comemos comíamos abrem abriam faço fiz teve tinha

Grammar in context 1 Cabral discovering Brazil and Pedro I declaring independence 2 How much it has changed its name

Unit 28

A 1 Chegaremos... 2 Visitaremos o local. 3 Iremos / faremos uma excursão ao Rio. 4 Iremos de compras. 5 Jantaremos... 6 Exploraremos a costa. 7 Veremos um espetáculo... 8 Partiremos.

B 1 Compraremos uma nova casa. 2 Onde está a Sara? Estará doente? 3 Amanhã vamos lavar o carro. 4 O avião chega (chegará) às 8.15. 5 Ficarei uma semana com eles. 6 Nunca irá ao teatro. 7 Vai visitar o João na semana que vem? 8 Esta tarde vão trabalhar no jardim. 9 Vai para Bahia. Estará quente? 10 Terminaremos a viagem em Lisboa.

Grammar in context 1 You will be offered a detailed visit to the wine lodges. 2 You will have the opportunity to look at hundreds of barrels of port. 3 You will be able to watch a video. 4 You will taste the excellent Port wines.

Unit 29

A 1 gostaria 2 compraria 3 daríamos 4 poderia 5 deveriam 6 veria

B 1 iriam 2 poderíamos 3 gostarias 4 ajudaria 5 adoraria 6 importaria 7 dariam 8 deverias 9 seria 10 iria

Grammar in context She would: buy a new Mercedes; visit her sister in the USA; go to the Costa Verde for a beach holiday; change her job – have her own shop; move house – to be nearer her parents; give her eldest son money to buy a motorbike; send her daughter to university in France; donate something to the church.

Unit 30

A 1 tenho 2 hás-de 3 tem 4 há 5 tem 6 *both* 7 têm 8 *both* 9 temos que 10 *both*

B 1 a true b false c true d true e false
2 ter: 2 haver: 2

Grammar in context (lit.) What is it that there is here?
It's the echo that there is here
Is there an echo here?
There is an echo here, there is.

Unit 31

A 1 construído 2 limpado 3 bebido 4 escrito 5 roto 6 furado 7 pago 8 preso

B The missing verb forms are: lavando lavado rir rido *laughed* vir *coming* vindo pagando *paying* pago cantar cantando *sung receiving* recebido *received* abrindo *opening* aberto ver visto *seen*

Grammar in context 1 the most authentic folklore show 2 processado, incluído, indicada

Unit 32

A 1 tens visto 2 tenho tido 3 tem feito 4 não tenho falado
5 não tem vindo 6 temos perdido 7 têm ido 8 tem trabalhado
9 não tem descansado 10 têm estado

B 1 e 2 g 3 b 4 h 5 a 6 d 7 f 8 c

Grammar in context He's been going to Brazil.

Unit 33

A 1 A tua filha tinha saído quando tu chegaste a casa. *Your
daughter went out. You arrived home. Your daughter had
(already) gone out when you arrived home.* 2 O 'show' tinha
começado quando entrámos no teatro. *The show began. We
entered the theatre. The show had begun when we entered the
theatre.* 3 Ele tinha pago a conta quando ela chamou o
empregado. *He paid the bill. She called the waiter. He had paid
the bill when she called the waiter.* 4 Nós tínhamos ido ao
centro quando tu telefonaste. *We went to town. You phoned.
We had gone to town when you phoned.* 5 Ela tinha feito o
jantar quando o programa começou. *She made the dinner. The
programme started. She had made the dinner when the
programme started.*

B 1 tinha comido 2 terão terminado 3 terias feito 4 teriam
podido 5 terá ido 6 teremos / tínhamos / teríamos pintado
7 tinha preparado 8 terá / teria acontecido

Unit 34

A 1 Estou a correr / correndo. 2 Estão a comer / comendo.
3 Está a pagar / pagando. 4 Estás a cozinhar / cozinhando.
5 Estamos a nadar / nadando. 6 Estão a sair / saindo. 7 Está a
ler / lendo. 8 Estão a jogar / jogando.

B 1 Estava a dormir. 2 Estava a jantar. 3 Estava a ver a TV.
4 Estava a beber água. 5 Estava a passear na rua. 6 Estava a
comer.

Grammar in context On approaching the host, should she
keep stopping to greet other friends?

Unit 35

A 1 c 2 h 3 e 4 j 5 a 6 g 7 f 8 i 9 b 10 d

B 1 e 2 a 3 c 4 f 5 b 6 d

Grammar in context 1 cover charge, if eaten or unusable 2 must be written in Portuguese

Unit 36

A 1 coma 2 limpe 3 falem 4 cantai 5 compre 6 abras 7 durmam 8 mintas 9 votai 10 escrevam

B 1 b 2 d 3 a 4 c

Grammar in context 1 speed limits 2 No 3 utilizar 4 every two hours

Unit 37

A 1 estou 2 vais 3 é 4 vimos 5 fizeram 6 pude 7 tiveste 8 dava 9 haviam 10 púnhamos

B Agora = podes, sei, hás, pode, fazes, dou, põe, vou, faz, estou, têm, dizemos

Ontem = foste, disse, viste, estivemos, pudeste, fiz, fostes, tive, houveram, vieste

Antigamente = estávamos, fazias, tinha, tínheis, haviam, punha

Grammar in context vir (venha), ver, ser (foi), poder (pode), ser

Unit 38

A 1 ✓ 2 ✓ 3 ✗ (sou) 4 ✗ (está) 5 ✓ 6 ✗ (é) 7 ✓ 8 ✓ 9 ✗ (estamos) 10 ✗ (é)

B 1 está 2 está 3 estamos 4 são 5 está 6 estão 7 é 8 estão 9 é 10 estou

Grammar in context 1 Se não fosse 2 não pode ser 3 é 4 o que seria

Unit 39

A 1 O jantar foi pago por / pela Maria. 2 Os lagos são adorados por todos os turistas. 3 A partida foi ganha pelo Benfica. 4 O carro foi levado pelo João. 5 Uma nova discoteca vai ser aberta. 6 O Banco do Brasil foi assaltado. 7 Os cães foram perdidos na floresta. 8 O trabalho foi feito por mim. 9 O concurso vai ser inaugurado por / pelo Luís Figo. **10** As senhoras foram acordadas pela música.

B **1** Está aberta. **2** Estão limpas. **3** Está assinado. **4** Está cortada. **5** Está feito. **6** Estão salvos. **7** Está fechado. **8** Estão pintadas.

Grammar in context **1** 713, by Abd-al-Aziz **2** D. Paio Peres Correia, Order of Santiago **3** Abd-al-Aziz conquistou Silves. D..... tomou Silves.

Unit 40

A **Present subjunctive:** pintes, pinte, pintemos, pintem, beba, bebas, beba, bebamos, bebam, parta, partas, parta, partamos, partam, faça, faças, faça, façamos, façam

Imperfect subjunctive: estudasse, estudasse, estudássemos, estudassem, corresse, corresses, corrêssemos, corressem, tivesse, tivesses, tivesse, tivéssemos, tivessem, dormisse, dormisses, dormisse, dormíssemos, dormissem

B **2** present / 3rd pers. plural / **fazer** / *to do, make* **3** imperfect / 1st pers. sing. / **trabalhar** / *to work* **4** future / 2nd pers. plural / **abrir** / *to open* **5** past perfect / 3rd pers. sing. / **beber** / *to drink* **6** future perfect / 1st pers. plural / **fazer** / *to do, make* **7** present / 2nd pers. sing. / **decidir** / *to decide* **8** future / 1st pers. plural / **comprar** / *to buy* **9** past perfect / 3rd pers. sing. / **doer** / *to hurt* **10** imperfect / 3rd pers. plural / **vir** / *to come*

Grammar in context voltar, espalhar, experimentar

Unit 41

A **1** sinta **2** fosse **3** façam **4** tivesse ganho **5** tivéssemos ido **6** mores **7** ver **8** saia **9** voltassem **10** estejam

B

A	C	O	N	S	E	L	H	A	R
B	C	D	E	E	G	H	R	L	I
L	M	N	O	N	Q	E	S	E	B
V	W	X	Y	T	Z	B	C	G	I
F	G	H	I	I	K	L	M	R	O
R	Q	R	D	R	U	V	W	A	R
E	A	R	A	S	I	C	E	R	P
M	K	G	M	N	O	P	Q	S	S
E	S	P	E	R	A	R	A	E	C
T	R	A	H	N	A	R	T	S	E

Grammar in context Solicitamos que = We *request that*...

Unit 42

A 1 É provável que eles venham mais tarde. 2 É verdade que tu trabalhas muito. 3 Achamos que a comida foi boa. 4 Vou ao Brasil, venha o que vier. 5 Era incrível que o Nélson falasse assim. 6 Era evidente que eles não tivessem feito isto. 7 É melhor não dizer nada. 8 Não penso que tu estejas doente.

B 1 h 2 c 3 j 4 e 5 g 6 b 7 i 8 d 9 f 10 a

Grammar in context wherever I might be

Unit 43

A Talvez + 1 haja... 2 estejamos... 3 durmamos... 4 se percam... 5 seja... 6 faça... 7 vejas... 8 diga... 9 queiras... 10 desça...

B 1 comas 2 tentem 3 diga 4 sejam 5 seja 6 poupem 7 seja 8 tenha

Grammar in context If you can't find the wine of the year you want

Unit 44

A 1 não custe muito 2 saiba reparar carros 3 possa pintar a casa 4 saiba conduzir 5 se dê bem com crianças 6 possa trabalhar de manhã 7 faça boa comida 8 trabalhe bem no jardim

Unit 45

A 1 gostas, d 2 chegávamos, h 3 tivesse, a 4 fossem, e
5 tivesses trazido, i 6 tivesse convidado, b 7 tiver, f 8 chover, j
9 morasses, c 10 tivéssemos reservado, g

B tiveres fosse ia deve tenho preciso fôssemos houver faço
fosse houvesse soubesse teria trazido voltar

Grammar in context If you find two symbols alike and a sun.

Unit 46

A Disse que: 1 gosta / gostava mais dos seus próprios
programas. 2 nunca perde / perdia o Telejornal, porque tem /
tinha de saber as notícias. 3 para ele, lá em Portugal, o melhor
apresentador tem / tinha de ser Jorge Gabriel. 4 Sempre vê / via
futebol, e que o dia anterior tinha visto um jogo. 5 não suporta
/ suportava os congressos…, e que no dia seguinte, se houvesse
este programa, desligava / desligaria a TV. 6 na opinião dele, o
melhor filme é / era… 7 se fosse para o bem de todos… dizia /
diria que sim.

Grammar in context 1 Rod Stewart 2 Manuel Vilarinho
3 Silvio Berlusconi 4 Ronaldo 5 Marisa Monte 6 Liam
Gallagher